Writings on Marx a

Barry. Vale

Also available from Amazon Kindle Publishing:

A History of the Church of England 1529 – 1662

A Brief Study of British Defence Policy

Barry's British History Blogs Compilation

Is Jaguar Land Rover Capable of Global Expansion?

Mythology vs Modernity

Public Diplomacy in Western Democracies

The Augustan Building Programme
The Influence of Changing Gender Roles during the 18th &
19thcenturies on the position of women in midwifery

Writings on the English Civil Wars - Three Kingdoms Torn Apart by
conflict
A Comparison of how the Thatcher Government and New Labour
attempted to bring back traditional family values

Contents

Preface

Introduction

The major ideas of Karl Marx and Friedrich Engels and their influence on working class movements of the mid – nineteenth century

'What is to be Done?', an improvement or perversion of Marx's theory of revolution?

Why did Marxism / Leninism affect Russia?

Marxism and Anarchism – Similarities and Differences

In considering the process of change in Russia and the Soviet Union over the whole period 1861 – 1964 how far can the Bolshevik Revolution be seen as the turning point?

The continuities in the Soviet relationship with East Germany (1945-1989)

The causes of the Soviet Union's Demise

The relationship between the May 4th Movement, the New Culture Movement and the Chinese Communist Party and assess the impact of this relationship on China's modernisation

In what ways and with what effects did the politicisation of culture contribute to the Chinese Communist Party's consolidation of power between the 1940s and the mid-1970s?

Preface

Karl Marx wrote a great deal during his own lifetime, and his works in turn led to countless articles, books and treatises that either supported or condemned his views. Marx himself presented arguments for socialism and then communism in his books and argued that history was on the side of communism. Theorists, revolutionaries, opponents and supporters of Marx have produced countless tomes since the 1840s to get their own perspectives and interpretations across.

The writing and ideas of Marx sometimes in conjunction with Engels caused much debate, devotion and indeed controversy in his lifetime and beyond.

The purpose of this work is to present some of the different writings I have completed concerning Marx and Marxism over the years. These should not in any way be considered a wholesale acceptance or rejection of all of Marx's writings though various analyses are presented.

Introduction

A spectre is haunting Europe – the spectre of Communism
(Marx & Engels, The Communist Manifesto)

Marxism is above all a method of analysis
(Leon Trotsky, quoted by Fraser, 1990 p. 270)

Karl Marx was a prolific writer and researcher who completed vast volumes of works and articles. With Engels and on his own he wrote about economics, politics, religions and societies with the overriding objective of promoting and eventually achieving Communism across the globe. Marx was convinced that his ideas would play a major role in spreading Communism everywhere beginning with the most technically and economically advanced nations and eventually the most backward of countries. He argued that history was on the side of the proletarians or industrial working classes. Revolution would come and with it Communism. Yet he was not always clear on how history made revolution inevitable.

Yet as the writings that follow demonstrate, Communism did not advance in the ways that Marx and Engels anticipated, or in the places that it was expected to advance. Communism has had adherents, detractors and has caused plenty of debate and conflict during and after the lifetime of Marx.

Both supporters and detractors would perhaps be sensible to take note of the quote from Trotsky.

Reference

Fraser, D (1990) Collins Concise Dictionary of Quotations, Harper Collins Publishers, London

The major ideas of Karl Marx and Friedrich Engels and their influence on working class movements of the mid – nineteenth century.

But what experience and history teach is this, that peoples and governments never learn from history
(G W Hegel – quoted in Fraser, 1990 p. 132)

Detailed below is a concise discussion concerning the major ideas of Karl Marx and Friedrich Engels in relation to their influence over working class movements in the mid – nineteenth century. In 1848, when Karl Marx and Friedrich Engels published the Communist Manifesto they intended to lead working class movements towards the inevitable victory of the Proletariat as they dubbed industrial workers, the belief at the very epicentre of their major ideas. It was a year durin which revolutions threatened to bring change across much of Europe y in the end did not. As will be examined they anticipated the total domination of the working class across the globe although various groups and organisations were influenced by their concepts to varying degrees.

Both Karl Marx and Friedrich Engels were originally from Prussia, the largest and most economically powerful country within the German Confederation although they moved to England as the British government allowed them to develop and then attempt to spread their major ideas without fear of repression. Prussia was one of the leading continental countries to industrialise after Belgium in the wake of Britain's industrialisation from the late eighteenth century (Hobsbawm, 1962 p. 119). As an aside, ironically, the Engels family also owned textile factories in Lancashire, allowing Marx access to actual members of the Proletariat. Engels was also using profits from his family's capitalist enterprises to fund research and writings designed to undermine and even overthrow that self and same system (Harvey, 200 p. 5). Karl Marx and Friedrich Engels were committed to the spreadin of their radical form of socialism subsequently referred to as communism before they had left their native Prussia, theoretically themselves strongly influenced by the writings of Karl Marx's philosophical inspiration, their former, University of Berlin tutor Georg Wilhelm Hegel (Hobsbawm, 1962 p. 122).

For Marx and Engels using Hegel's complex dialectic approach to explain economics, history, and also societies was essential in the contention central to the message of the Communist Manifesto - that the Proletariat would ultimately triumph over all other classes. They also encouraged the working class movements of mid – nineteenth century to co – operate with each other in order to co – ordinate their activities to bring forward the collapse of the non – Proletarian classes. After all by untying the working class movements and their Proletarian members had to paraphrase the Communist Manifesto had nothing to lose but their chains, and would literally inherit the Earth. Yet Marxist groups even at this stage found it difficult to interest workers in their own country to consider what was happening to fellow workers across Europe let alone form an all powerful international organisation to spread Communism (Eatwell & Wright, 2003 p.279).

The major ideas of Karl Marx and Friedrich Engels influenced working class movements of the mid - nineteenth century by providing these groups with the theoretical framework and terminology to understand their respective economies, history, politics, and also societies. It was the publicly expressed intention of Marxist ideology to provide working class movements with a long – term perspective of class conflicts, ultimately replacing the inadequate or limited earlier socialist or social democratic ideas put forward by more moderate groups and individuals. They were advocating full blown socialism instead of limited trade unionism or social democracy that would not overturn existing feudal or capitalist social orders (Harvey, 2003 p. 11).

Moderate social democracy was a concept, which Karl Marx and Friedrich Engels simply could not abide with, as it protected the status quo and would not provide workers with any benefits while preventing their rise to power. Indeed Karl Marx and Friedrich Engels within their major ideas went out of their way to criticise the moderate forms of socialism and social democracy as nothing better than Utopian socialism, which prevented working class movements from achieving Proletarian paradises upon Earth. Karl Marx and Friedrich Engels frequently argued that working class movements needed to do a whole lot more than merely campaign for higher wages, fewer working hours, and more tolerable working conditions (Cobden, 1968 p.44). Instead the workers had to work together to achieve the Communist system that would transform all economies and societies (Hobsbawm, 1962 p. 123).

Instead the working class movements of the mid nineteenth century according to Karl Marx and Friedrich Engels should have aimed towards the overthrow of capitalism, and even feudalism in backward countries such as Russia (Hosking, 2001 p. 360) Utopian socialists and social democrats lacked the nerve to attempt to win the class struggle and thereby secure control of the means of production for the Proletariat. The impact of Karl Marx and Friedrich Engels on working class movements was not the same everywhere. In the nineteenth century the majority of working class movements were divided as to whether or not the major Marxist ideas such as alienation, the class struggle, and historical materialism should influence or even dominate their over all economic, political, and social objectives (Hobsbawm, 1962 p. 127).

In many respects the major ideas of Karl Marx and Friedrich Engels did not influence the working class movements of mid – nineteenth century as much as they would have liked. They had been confident that communism had human history upon its side and that capitalism would be replaced by communism in the same way that capitalism itself had replaced feudalism. Karl Marx and Friedrich Engels had noted that inevitable economic and social changes affected countries and regions a different speeds, with the most advanced experiencing such transformations first. Therefore logically enough Karl Marx and Friedrich Engels had argued that communism would be achieved soone in the countries in which capitalism had developed the most, namely Britain, France, Prussia, and even the United States (Harvey, 2003 p. 15).

As capitalism advanced the level of alienation experienced by the Proletariat would lead to revolution, as workers would successfully mastermind the capture of the means of economic production. Karl Mar and Friedrich Engels assumed that contemporary working class movements would eventually adopt the strategies put forward in their major ideas to gain complete economic and political control of their respective societies. With hindsight they misjudged the motivations of working class movements and the determination of the capitalist ruling classes to maintain their dominant positions (Hobsbawm, 1975 p. 18). Greed and self preservation are arguably factors, which can explain why the proletarians frequently fail to work to overthrow capitalism and replace it with socialism or ultimately Communism (Eatwell & Wright, 2003 p. 283).

Much to the chagrin of Karl Marx and Friedrich Engels the working class movements of mid – nineteenth century Britain were moderate in beliefs and strategies, they generally favoured evolutionary changes, and were mainly concerned with increasing wage levels. British workers wanted to avoid poverty rather overthrow the capitalist system itself. At the time Karl Marx and Friedrich Engels believed France offered better prospects for Proletarian triumph. French working class movements were considered capable of launching further revolutionary waves similar in magnitude to those of 1789, 1830, and 1848 (Wheen, 1999 p. 382).

Ironically enough the next serious attempted revolution in France followed in the wake of defeat in the Franco – Prussian War of 1870 – 1871. Yet the Marxists were in the end unable to replace the Second empire with a Communist republic and not able to gain power in the Third Republic. French Marxists did not even control all of the trade unions (Cobden, 1968 p. 45). The rapid industrialization of Prussia and to a lesser extent other German states started to increase the number of recruits available to join working class movements and thus have an impact upon politics inside the German Confederation. Of course been Prussians Karl Marx and Friedrich Engels were enthusiastic about spreading their major ideas to Prussia whilst in their British exile. In the middle of the nineteenth century the Prussian authorities were certainly concerned that the influence of the major ideas of Karl Marx and Friedrich Engels could de - stabilize their country. Thus Berlin repeatedly requested that the British government should censor Marx and Engels, or send them back to be imprisoned in Prussia. This the British authorities never did (Eatwell & Wright, 2003 p. 280).

The unwillingness of British working class movements to embrace any of the major ideas of Karl Marx and Friedrich Engels during the mid – nineteenth century was in stark contrast to their influence on the European mainland. French working class movements during this period often adopted Marxist approaches, policies, and terms although their level of orthodoxy did not always please Karl Marx and Friedrich Engels. The Prussian socialists especially Karl Kautsky regarded the key elements of the major ideas of Karl Marx and Friedrich Engels to gain power democratically. The popularity of the Prussian social democrats increased still further after German unification in 1871 (Hobsbawm, 1975 p. 17). Working class movements amongst the stateless Poles and those in Tsarist Russia were undeniably influenced by the major ideas of Karl Marx and Friedrich Engels. The Poles had to endure occupation by the Austrians, the Prussians, and the Russians. Some Poles joined Austrian, Prussian, or Russian working class movements, whilst others joined exclusively Polish socialist movements. The few working class movements within the Russian Empire were strongly influenced by the major ideas of Karl Marx and Friedrich Engels. However due to the notable backwardness of the Russian economy, and the attentions of the Tsarist secret police they remained weak during the mid – nineteenth period (Hosking, 2001 p. 361).

Conclusions

The major ideas of Karl Marx and Friedrich Engels were therefore highly important in the development of socialism and influenced working class movements in the mid – nineteenth century and beyond. Not only did it influence these movements it frequently caused responses from those that held economic, political and social power. Their major ideas such as alienation, historical materialism, and the class struggle between capitalism and communism influenced working class movements to either support or reject Marxist ideology. Over all the major ideas of Karl Marx and Friedrich Engels had very little influence over working class movements in Britain, yet had a greater impact on such movements in France, Prussia, and more surprisingly Russia. Tsarist Russia lacked the proletarian workers that could be found in Britain, France, Prussia and even Belgium. Although the Tsarist authorities would eventually attempt to modernise the empire even by the start of the First World War the number of working class people was very limited compared to Western Europe.

Bibliography

Cobden, A (1968) A History of Modern France, Part 3 1871 – 1962, Pelican, London

Eatwell R & Wright A (2003) Contemporary Political Ideologies 2nd edition, Continuum, Stroud

Fraser, D (1990) Collins Concise Dictionary of Quotations, Harper Collins Publishers, London

Harvey R, (2003) Comrades – the rise and fall of World Communism, John Murray, London

Hobsbawm, E (1962) The Age of Revolution 1789 – 1848, Weidenfeld & Nicholson, London

Hobsbawm, E (1975) The Age of Capital 1848 – 1875 , Weidenfeld & Nicholson, London

Hosking, G (2001) Russia and the Russians – A History from Rus to the Russian Federation, Allen Lane, London

Wheen F, (1999) Karl Marx, 4th Estate, London

'What is to be Done?', an improvement or perversion of Marx's theory of revolution?

A cardinal tenet of the revolutionary movement up to the early 1890s had been that Marx's teaching on historical evolution did not apply to Russia
(Hosking, 2001 p. 360)

The discussion below debates whether or not Lenin in his seminal work 'What is to be Done?' improved or in fact perverted Marx's theory of revolution. Karl Marx had put forward his theory of revolution most notably in the Communist Manifesto that he originally co-wrote with Frederick Engels in 1848. Karl Marx's theory of revolution put forward the notion that communist revolutions would happen eventually, these revolutions would not be stopped, and indeed such events are inevitable. Karl Marx and Frederick Engels were able to attract the support of people towards their ideas of communism, class war, and revolutions, yet Marx himself never came up with practical suggestions for achieving proletarian revolutions and making them a reality. After Karl Marx died his many theories were mainly co-ordinated into a more coherent doctrine by Frederick Engels as well as Karl Kautsky to achieve communism. Vladimir Lenin came to believe that a different approach was needed to turn Marxist revolution into a reality. 'What is to be Done?' was Vladimir Lenin's blueprint for the carrying out of a proletarian seizure of power, which attracted supporters and also detractors. Lenin's supporters argued that he was merely allowing Marxism to fulfil its destiny, detractors that he was perverting all that Marx had stood for.

In all his writings Karl Marx had implied that proletarian revolutions would be inevitable and the proletariat would become the ruling class in every country in the world. These revolutions would take place in the most advanced economies and societies before eventually taking place the least advanced ones. Karl Marx based his theory of revolution on Hegelian concepts of the dialectic and also the inevitable curse of human history (Eatwell & Wright, 2003 p. 114). According to Marx therefore communism would invariably and ultimately be the final outcome of human economic and social development. Marx's theory of revolution was thus deterministic in its nature, as he argued that the economies and societies of countries had to reach a certain stage of development before the proletariat revolutions could actually take place (James, 2003 p. 60)

For Marx the most advanced countries such as Britain, France, and his native Prussia / Germany would be ready for, and experience their proletarian revolutions before the more backward countries like China, and Tsarist Russia (Hobsbawm, 1994 p. 27). Marx was aware that his ideas had attracted supporters in Russia such as Lenin yet expected them to wait for their revolution to happen when the time was right. Whilst Marx contended that proletarian revolutions could not be avoided or averted his theory of revolution did not given any indication of when such revolutions would actually occur except for vague references to when the economic and social conditions and the time was right (Harvey, 2003 p. 32). Marx anticipated that the most advanced capitalist countries in general, and Britain in particular would be only decades away from their proletarian revolution as opposed to backward countries like Tsarist Russia that were potentially two or three centuries away from having successful proletarian revolutions of their own. The thing that Marx's theory of revolution neglected to mention in suitable depth was how proletarian revolutions would be achieved, he was just convinced that they would happen in every country at some point in time due to the ways in, which economies and societies developed (Eatwell & Wright, 2003 p. 110). There was therefore plenty of scope for Lenin to improve or pervert Marx's theory of revolution in 'What is to be Done?' as the theory itself was vague and also open to different interpretations of its meaning and how it would be fulfilled (Lenin, 1902 p 1).

The writings of Karl Marx had done a great deal to spread the ideological and political concepts of socialism, communism, as well as what became known as Marxism. Indeed Marx had produced copious amounts of analysis concerning the development and the functioning of the capitalist system, particularly in the meticulously researched 'Das Kapital', which claim to highlight the weaknesses of the capitalist modes of economic production (James, 2003 p. 60). Besides as far as Marx was concerned capitalism would sow the seeds of its own destruction just as feudalism had unintentionally led to the emergence of capitalism itself. However it would possible for feudalism, capitalism, and communism to exist at the same time as countries develop at different rates. Those that wanted to experience a proletarian revolution just had to wait for one, if they fortunate enough to live in one of the most advanced countries they would probably not have to wait too long (Wheen, 1999 p. 385).

It can be plausibly argued that with 'What is to be Done?' Lenin was able to improve upon Marx's theory of revolution. With the writing of 'What is to be Done?' Lenin gave a greater amount of consideration to the practical steps that were needed to bring about proletarian revolutio as soon as possible rather than waiting for decades or even centuries fo one to occur once all the predetermined conditions fell into place. Marx's theory of revolution was for the patient and those that were safe from persecution for their political beliefs; Lenin was neither patient no felt safe from the Tsarist authorities and secret police. 'What is to be Done?' was an improvement upon the ideas of Marx concerning revolution as it was meant as a blueprint for Marxist parties everywhere to go out and achieve their own revolutions in the present or the near future. That was better than doing nothing apart from waiting for revolutions to start of their own accord. Lenin contended that proletarian revolution could be achieved when capitalism showed weaknesses, or indeed in times of crisis as that would be apparent befor capitalism reached the point of its own collapse. Lenin argued that all Marxist parties had to search for weaknesses in capitalism and then take advantage of all opportunities that are identified to launch proletarian revolutions. Other radical Marxist such as Rosa Luxemburg shared Lenin's ideas about bringing about revolution in the present (Luxemburg).

'What is to be Done?' was thus a considerable improvement upon Karl Marx's theory of revolution as it urged that all serious Marxist parties and political organisations to adopt a proactive approach or strategy towards achieving revolutions across the globe. Proactive actions rathe than passively waiting for human history to take it are proper, and also long drawn out course (James, 2003 p. 62). Revolutionary opportunitie had to be taken whenever, or wherever they have arisen or existed as such chances would not last for too long, which would allow for the reactionary forces of capitalism to resist them. Changes in more backward countries were also resisted by the old feudal order, and have the time to take steps to avoid revolutions in the first place. Lenin argued that it did not matter where or when the opportunities for successful proletarian revolutions occurred just as long as the relevant Marxist party was able to take full economic, political, and social contr of their own country. One successful proletarian revolution could certainly act as a catalyst for further successful revolutions in other countries. As far as Lenin was concerned the strategies that he put forward were theoretically sound as well as being pragmatic, and equated to giving human history a substantial helping hand (Woodruff, 2005 p. 200).

Lenin had improved on Marx's theory of revolution, as 'What is to be Done?' was more of a systematic and coherent work that happened to be more explicit than Marx had been in his writing. Whilst Marx had painstakingly analysed the weaknesses of, and the inconsistencies contained within the capitalist system he had not provided guidance on how to overthrow capitalism to bring about communism via revolution (Lichtheim). On the other hand, Lenin did suggest ways to achieve revolution and practical methods for the overthrowing of capitalism to bring about communism ahead of schedule whether it was newly emerging as it was in Tsarist Russia, or more firmly established as it was in Britain, France, and Germany (Lenin, 1902 p. 2). Lenin decided to write 'What is to be Done?' to suggest ways in which revolutions could be launched rather than just happen as a means to overcome the problems presented by the backwardness of Russia and to explain why the more advanced countries had not experienced proletarian revolutions (Wheen, 1999 p. 386). Lenin argued that the strategies and tactics he put forward in 'What is to be Done?' were the only effective means of fulfilling Marx's dreams of achieving successful proletarian revolution and destroying the capitalist system before it enslaved the proletariat forever. Lenin also rejected the peaceful and the constitutional paths to power as preferred by moderate Marxist parties such as the SPD in Germany, and the non-Marxist Labour Party in Britain. Lenin contended that socialism or communism achieved peacefully in liberal democracies would not be a long lasting achievement as capitalist parties could easily reverse any changes simply by winning subsequent elections (Woodruff, 2005 p. 201).

There were of course arguments that the ideas put forward by Lenin in 'What is to be Done?' perverted Marx's theory of revolution. Indeed that Lenin's ideas turned the theory completely on it's head. Orthodox Marxists around the time that 'What is to be Done?' was written and indeed until the October Revolution itself argued that Lenin was actually decreasing the chances of a successful communist revolution taking place at all (Lichtheim). The critics of Lenin argued that the danger of applying the strategies and tactics that Lenin favoured was that they recommended then accelerated the path towards a proletarian revolution without there been any significant numbers of the proletariat being involved in carrying it out. The premature launching of a revolution attempt could indeed be highly detrimental for the long-term prospects of a successful proletarian revolution, as failure could strengthen the forces of repression. There was no need to take excessive risks when all of human history was working towards the final victory of the proletaria in any case (Eatwell & Wright, 2003 p. 113).

The more orthodox Marxists argued that it was their duty to educate the proletariat in their respective countries to embrace the concepts of communism and work towards achieving revolution as well as winning the class war when the moment was right to do so. Lenin's insistence that his party should carry out a revolution whenever and wherever it could irrespective of the readiness or even the support of the majority of the Russian proletariat perverted Marx's theory of revolution (Harvey, 2003 p. 31). Lenin would further enrage his critics by working towards gaining the support of the Russian peasants in order to take power whenever the opportunity arose to do so. After all the vast majority of the Russian population at the start of the 20th century was made up of illiterate peasants. With only very small numbers of the middle classes and even fewer members of the proletariat, it made the prospects for a successful revolution appear to be very remote indeed. Thus Tsarist Russia according to Marx's own ideas about revolution would take decades at least to have a proletariat large enough to successfully take power (James, 2003 p. 62).

There were also arguments that Lenin's 'What is to be Done?' perverted Marx's theory of revolution as it would bring about regimes if it proved to be a successful strategy that were not truly proletarian or communist in their composition and their actual policies. The strategies and the tactics favoured by Lenin in 'What is to be Done?' would lead to nominally proletarian regimes that did not have any or only a few members of the proletariat within their ranks. The Leninist approach would not lead to the foundation of authentic Marxist states, only to regimes that pretended to be communist. By successfully carrying out the policies included within 'What is to be Done?' Lenin would create a dictatorship that would only cater for the needs of the party leadership rather than looking after the interests of the proletariat. The other problem was that if successful Lenin would have to carry out economic policies that would greatly expand the size of the proletariat after gaining power otherwise the communist regime would only rule to help itself (Hobsbawm, 1994 p. 29).

Therefore it can be concluded that Lenin's 'What is to be Done?' was an over al improvement over Karl Marx's theory of revolution. The strategies and tactics put forward within Lenin's 'What is to be Done?' were certainly significantly different from those supported by other Marxists such as Frederick Engels, Karl Kautsky, and the moderate leadership of the SPD in Germany. The main problem when deciding upon the validity of Lenin's strategies and tactics was that the majority of Marx's theories were either vague or down right contradictory. This lack of coherence meant that there were numerous different theories and opinions that Marxist groups and thinkers could hold that were totally opposite from each other, yet all could still claim to be true Marxists. There were a great deal of divergent political theories, and proposed policies that involved frequently impassioned debates between Marxist groups, parties, individuals, and factions. With 'What is to be Done?' Lenin certainly turned fundamental aspects of Marxism upon their head, whilst demonstrating an astute understanding of the internal situation in Russia in order to launch a successful revolution there.

Bibliography

Eatwell R & Wright A (2003) Contemporary Political Ideologies 2nd
Edition, Continuum, London
Harvey R, (2003) Comrades – the rise and fall of World Communism,
John Murray, London
Hobsbawm, E (1994) Age of Extremes, the Short Twentieth Century
1914-1991, Michael Joseph, London

Hosking, G (2001) Russia and the Russians – A History from Rus to th
Russian Federation, Allen Lane, London

James, H (2003) Europe Reborn – A History, 1914 – 2000, Pearson
Longman, Harlow
Lenin, (1902) 'What is to be Done?'
Lichtheim G, 'Marxism'
Luxemburg R, 'The Russian Revolution: Leninism or Marxism'
Wheen F, (1999) Karl Marx, 4th Estate, London
Woodruff W, (2005) A concise history of the Modern World, Abacus,
London

Why did Marxism / Leninism affect Russia?

"It speedily became evident that these Bolshevik socialists were men of a very different quality," (Wells, 1944 p. 259).

There are various reasons and factors that can be used to explain the affect that Marxism / Leninism had upon Russia and why it was to achieve that affect. Some of these explanations are based around the actions of the Bolshevik Party that seized power in October 1917 and did not formally relinquish that power until the dissolution of the Soviet Union in 1991. Other reasons are based around factors that were not directly caused by the Bolshevik Party yet it was able to use them to its own advantage to affect Russia. Marxism / Leninism would become the official ideology of the Soviet Union which was basically Tsarist Russia shorn of Finland, Poland and for a time the Baltic States. Yet history and politics could have been completely different without the combination that enabled Marxism / Leninism to affect Russia with some spectacular and arguably some disastrous results. At the end there will be a discussion of the books used as references for this work and their respective value and merit.

Lenin had pledged that he would bring about the first Marxist State at the funeral of Karl Marx's daughter and son in law in 1911. Few took him seriously although events would vindicate his confidence (Wheen, 1999, p. 386). To start with the Bolshevik Party was a Marxist party that few outside the Tsarist secret police took seriously or knew that they existed. They were a splinter from the Russian Social Democratic Labour Party that seemed to spend more time arguing with the other half of that defunct party, the Mensheviks rather than destroying the imperial government through a successful socialist revolution (Longley 1980 p.8). Karl Marx and Frederick Engels had predicted that socialist revolutions would only occur in advanced capitalist countries such as Britain, Germany and the US not in backward Tsarist Russia. Russian industry had started to develop yet had not produced enough proletariat workers for most Marxists to expect a communist revolution. Lenin however believed that revolution in Russia was possible so long as the Bolshevik party could not gain support from the proletariat but the peasants that constituted the vast majority of the population as well (Hobsbawm, 1994 p. 25).

Although Marx had preached that time was on the side of the workers and that history would witness their final triumph over capitalism, Lenin was of the opinion that history needed to be made rather than just waited for. Marxism/Leninism was based on the promise that the Bolshevik party had to become the vanguard of the proletariat and achieve power in its name via revolutionary struggle. Lenin was the driving force behind the Bolshevik party he guided its strategy, ideology and was its undisputed leader. Without Lenin there would have been no Leninism and probably no Marxism in Russia. However, Lenin was only able to take power due to some opportunities that unexpectedly came along and gave the Bolshevik party its chance to enforce Marxism/Leninism on Russia (Roberts, 1996 p. 430).

Russia had seemed to overcoming the threat of a successful revolution, as the internal political and security situation seemed to have settled down after the 1905 revolution. That revolution had been a sign of things to come as it was set off as a result of defeat against Japan during the war of 1904-05. Instead of a straightforward victory, the Russian army was heavily defeated in Korea and Manchuria whilst the once proud Russian navy was virtually destroyed. Even such a short war had put a strain on the Russian economy and shown it to be militarily ineffective despite the size of its army. The Tzar did nothing to rectify the shortcomings of the Russian army to the country's detriment yet to the advantage of revolutionary organisations (Roberts, 1996 p. 428). The economic reforms of Stolypin seemed to restore stability and enhance industrial development although he advised the Tzar to avoid further wars. One consequence of the 1905 revolution had been the creation of Russia's first parliament, the Duma that in reality took no power from the Tsarist autocracy. Only the collapse of that power woul make way for successful revolution (Hobsbawm, 1994 p.58).

The immaturity of Russian political parties in the democratic process, the limited franchise and power of the Duma would assist the affect tha Marxism / Leninism had on Russia. That is because the opponents of th Bolsheviks could not offer a strong alternative of a constitutional monarchy or liberal republic. The Communist Party also had party members that were given jobs to get the civil service, the police and the army functioning again after the disruption caused by war and revolution. Hobsbawm mentions that the experience of underground activity against the Tsarist and Provisional governments had made the Communists more determined and effective than their opponents

(Hobsbawm, 1994 p.58).

The great catalyst for revolutionary change and a strong factor in Marxism / Leninism having the profound affect on Russia that it did was the First World War which wrought havoc on the old order of Europe. Despite the embarrassing defeat of 1904-05, Russia remained on paper as much as in reality a great power that could have altered the balance of power in Europe. If the war had been short and victorious than perhaps things would have been different and the monarchy could have survived and successfully avoided revolution. The outbreak of war as in much of Europe was greeted with popular enthusiasm and support for the imperial regime (Hobsbawm, 1994 p.58). Russia was allied to France and its old rival Britain and also considered itself the protector of the Slavic peoples of Central and Eastern Europe, especially Serbia (Marix Evans, 2002, p. 12).

Germany had feared the sheer size of the Russian army rather than its quality. That fear led to the creation of the S P that came very close to quickly knocking France out of the war and thus allowing the Germans to concentrate on defeating Russia. The Russians had high expectations of success in August 1914 when they attempted to invade Germany. However these hopes were dashed when they were routed at Tannenberg. After that the Russian army never regained the initiative. Even with only 20 % of the German army being available on the Eastern Front the Russians were completely outclassed (Colvin, 2003 p.238). Russian loses were staggering at least 130,000 casualties with the additional loss of between 180-500 heavy guns. Worse still was the fact that Russia could not replace the loss of its finest men and equipment as it lacked the ability to adequately train replacements and the industrial capacity to replace lost equipment (Colvin, 2003, p. 244).

Nicholas II staked the future of the Romanov dynasty upon the successful outcome of the First World War. Given the weaknesses of the Russian economy, it's backward industries and it's chronically under equipped and led army that was a recipe for disaster. To make things worse Nicholas II compounded that error by making himself commander in chief of the army and thus directly to blame for its failures. Being away from Petrograd much of the time meant he was not fully aware of events and unable to change policies to avert trouble. As Nicholas II was ultimately responsible for Russian policy he could have stayed out of the First World War and done much to prevent revolution and civil war.

Castleden was not the first and will not be the last to suggest that the incompetence of the Tsarist government allowed Marxism / Leninism to affect Russia (Castleden, 2005 p.216).

Support for the government crumbled away as the war went from bad to worse meaning more extreme ideas such as Marxism / Leninism were seen as alternatives to the Tsarist regime. War time conditions meant civilians had to survive on lower rations. Radical groups and parties such as the Bolsheviks offered the hope of food and promised to end the war attracting support from workers, peasants and workers. Both agricultural and industrial output declined as men left for the army and were not replaced. Weapons shortages at the front when combined with food and fuel shortages brought Russia to the brink of revolution (Hobsbawm, 1994 p.58).

The entry of Turkey into the First World War had prevented the British and French supplying the Russian war effort, making it harder for the regime to stay in the war and survive its intense hardships. The failure of the Gallipoli offensive to knock Turkey out of the war meant that the Russians were in serious risk of losing the war. Marix Evans mentions that Turkey got in the way of the British and French keeping the Russians in the war as well as threatening their oil supplies (Marix Evans, 2002 p.111). The severity of the 1916 winter brought things to a head contributing to the strikes in Petrograd that escalated into the February Revolution and the replacement of the autocracy by the Provisional Government. The Provisional Government played into the hands of the Bolsheviks with the decision to continue fighting in the war. That error allowed Lenin and the Bolsheviks to make their propaganda more effective whilst planning a coup or revolution at the earliest opportune moment. Once Lenin returned from exile via Germany he and Leon Trotsky started the process of preparing their revolution by taking over workers, peasants and soldiers soviets, pledging bread, peace and land to maximise their support. Marxism / Leninism was able to affect Russia due to the astuteness that Lenin and Trotsky displayed during 1917 on the way towards, during and after the October Revolution (Lindley, 1980 p.7).

Marxism / Leninism had an affect on Russia as the Bolsheviks were able to take over the Russian state following the October Revolution and tightened that control during the Russian Civil War. Lenin authorised the use of secret police, executions and war communism during the civil war; the ruthlessness of the new regime allowed it to survive. Trotsky formed the Red Army that won the civil war, which was then used to control the Soviet Union in the name of the Communist Party. The Communists promoted Marxism / Leninism in schools farms, in factories and in the Red Army. The people of the Soviet Union were indoctrinated with Marxism / Leninism and faced repressive measures if they acted against Marxism / Leninism and the first state too openly proclaim it. During Stalin's period of office as General Secretary of the Communist Party of the Soviet Union, Marxism / Leninism provided the ideological context for brutally imposed collectivisation and industrialisation even if it did not excuse his bloody purges, mass deportations and murders (Castleden, 2005 p. 245).

Marxism / Leninism in theory had extolled the virtues of the differing nationalities within the Soviet Union in an effort to keep control over the different parts of the Russian empire that sought independence after the collapse of the monarchy. The Red Army had ended the Ukraine's brief independence, been unable to regain Finland and the Baltic States whilst suffering defeat against Poland. Although Stalin was a Georgian himself brutally suppressed nationalism in the Soviet republics outside of Russia itself. This would prove especially the case in his native Georgia and the second largest republic within the Soviet Union, the Ukraine. Therefore Marxism / Leninism affected Russia by keeping the majority of the old Tsarist Empire intact in a different form until the final collapse of the Soviet Union in 1991. Instead of the monarchy binding the empire together the official ideology of Marxism / Leninism bound the Soviet Union together. Stalin was responsible for the executions, deportations or simply leaving millions of non-Russian nationalists to starve to death. He was more of a Russian imperialist than any Tzar had ever been with the facility to use as much state controlled terror as he considered apt to keep the Soviet Union under his control (Bullock, 1991, pp 30-01).

Stalin arguably took the Soviet Union in a different direction than Lenin had intended to, or so those that wish to clear Lenin of any blame for the excesses of the Stalin regime would claim. Lenin's premature death meant that different factions within the Communist Party would claim to be acting in his name with their own version of Marxism / Leninism. Even before the outcomes of those power struggles was decided Lenin was made the focal point of the Soviet states propaganda and education. Thus Marxism / Leninism had an impact on Russia due to the cult of personality the Communist Party developed around Lenin after his death. In the Soviet Union, Lenin's name and image were everywhere. All his successors claimed that everything they did was done in his nam and that is how he would have done things when he was living (Lindley 1980 p.7). The cult of Lenin began in earnest after his funeral and with Stalin later carrying out all his policies in the name of Marxism / Leninism. It was Stalin that made Marxism / Leninism affects upon Russia and the rest of the Soviet Union more deeply than may otherwis have been the case (Bullock, 1991 pp.148-49).

Trotsky had seemed the most likely to succeed Lenin although he died without nominating his own successor, yet Trotsky would lose that power struggle with Stalin. Stalin had longer to make Marxism / Leninism than any other Communist leader especially with the dire consequences of some of his policies such as collectivisation. Stalin made the position of General Secretary of the Communist Party the mo powerful position in the Soviet Union. Stalin completely outmanoeuvre his rivals to gain total control of party and state. Stalin would promote many of his loyalists followers within both party and state. The Stalini era increased the link between party membership and being successful a work, within the civil service and the armed forces providing individua could avoid becoming victims of the purges (Pereira, 1992 p. 16). Stali would change the ethnic make up of the Soviet Union by deporting ove a million Tartars and Chechens amongst other ethnic groups to the gulags. In the name of Marxism / Leninism Stalin tried to ethnically cleanse the Soviet Union to ensure loyalty to his regime. Stalin therefor affected Russia and the other former Soviet republics by laying the foundations for future ethnic disputes such as the Chechen campaigns for independence (Castleden, 2005 p.247).

Marxism / Leninism was a term originally used by Stalin in order if not to explain his policies to at least justify their consequences. Humanity was controlled by 'uncontrollable social forces' that still needed to be enacted by leaders with the rare qualities of Lenin and his only viable successor Stalin. Stalin could explain his U-turns in domestic and foreign policy by keeping true to the essence of Marxism / Leninism. Such U-turns included initially supporting the New Economic Policy and then adopting collectivisation and industrialisation after defeating his rivals or Stalin's unsuccessful attempts to counter the fascist powers in the 1930s prior to signing the Nazi-Soviet Pact in 1939. Stalin was n a man troubled by contradictions or paradox. The strength of the regim and his grip on power came ahead of any ideological consideration (Eatwell & Wright, 2003 p. 118). All of Stalin's successors until Gorbachev stressed their devotion to Marxism / Leninism as the guiding ideology of the Soviet Union and the centrality of the Communist Party to the Soviet state. Gorbachev tried to reform the Soviet economy and open up its society. Yet by removing the control of the Communist Party he only succeeded in accelerating the collapse of the Soviet Union. Gorbachev proved Lenin and Stalin to be correct, the Soviet Union could not Marxism / Leninism to bind it together (Hobsbawm, 1994 p.498). The Soviet era had left behind a bloody legacy, an estimated 20 million deaths that resulted from Stalin's excesses on top of the estimated 8.8 million deaths from the Russian Civil War (Castleden, 2005 p.9). Soviet losses in the Second World War were horrendous at around 20 million due to Hitler's genocidal policies though the Stalinist regime survived much greater damages than the Imperial regime did not (Bullock, 1991 p. 1086).

Therefore Marxism / Leninism affected Russia because it was enforced upon the majority of the population following the Bolsheviks seizure of power in October 1917 and the consolidation of that power following their victory in the Russian Civil War. The Bolsheviks had originally been able to take power in Russia due not only to their strengths and strategy but also the weaknesses and mistakes of their immediate predecessors the autocracy of Nicholas II and short-lived Provisional Government. Perhaps the main reasons that Marxism / Leninism had an affect on Russia were the disastrous consequences of the First World War upon the Imperial regime. Defeat in the war with Japan had brought about the 1905 Revolution yet the government had done very little to modernise the army or improve the quality of its men and officers bearing in mind that the highly effective German army was it most likely adversary. Defeat at Tannenberg got the Russians off to a disastrous start to the war made worse when their allies were unable to succeed at Gallipoli in opening supply routes to reinforce the Russian army and its over-stretched industry. Worsening wartime conditions led to the collapse of the Tsarist regime in February 1917 yet staying in the war hampered the chances of the Provisional Government surviving. Lenin and Trotsky planned the successful October Revolution that brought the Communists to power yet had to rebuild the Tsarist state to win the Russian Civil War and secure its own future. Marxism / Leninism as such was the concept of Joseph Stalin who used it to justify the bloody consequences of collectivisation, industrialisation and his purges. Stalin made sure Marxism / Leninism affected the entire Soviet Union and no just Russia. In a sense industrialisation saved Russia following the German invasion of 1941. It survived dire loses and to turn the tide with victories at Stalingrad and Kursk. Above all the concepts of Marxism / Leninism affected Russia as it bound it to the other republics of the Soviet Union and delayed the break up of the Russian Empire for 75 years.

Bibliography

Bullock A (1991) Hitler and Stalin – Parallel Lives, Harper Collins, London

Castleden R (2005) The World's Most Evil People, Time Warner Books, London and New York

Colvin J (2003) Decisive Battles – Over 20 key naval and military encounters from 480 BC to 1943, Headline Book Publishing, London

Eatwell, R. & Wright, A (2003) Contemporary Political Ideologies 2nd Edition, Continuum, London

Hobsbawm, E (1994) Age of Extremes, the Short Twentieth Century 1914-1991, Michael Joseph, London

Longley J D – Makers of the Twentieth Century: Lenin, History Today, Volume 30, Issue 4, April 1980

Marix Evans M (2002) Over the Top – Great Battles of the First World War

Pereira N – Stalin and the Communist Party in the 1920s, History Today

Roberts J M (1995) A History of Europe, Penguin Books, London

Wells H G (1944) A Short History of the World, Pelican Books, Hammondsworth and New York

Wheen F (1999) Karl Marx, Fourth Estate Publications, London

Marxism and Anarchism – Similarities and Differences

There are some elements of Marxism and Anarchism that could be considered to be similar to each other and other aspects over, which these political ideologies clearly differ. When it comes to providing a critique of liberal philosophy and it's ideological justification of the capitalist system they have similar and different arguments against liberal philosophy. These ideologies are opposed to capitalism and have been working towards it's overthrow since the 19th century. Arguably Anarchism is working to a point where is no formal state, though that does not mean that Marxists and Anarchist would not cooperate if they believed that this was the best way to achieve mutual objectives. Whilst there have been and officially there are still Marxist states no government has ever claimed to be an Anarchist state as that would a paradoxical statement. The supporters of Marxism and Anarchism have tended to use similar terms when criticising liberal philosophy, such as discussing it's failure to admit that capitalism alienates all of those who do not benefit from the wealth that it generates. The reasons why there are similarities and differences between Marxism and Anarchism will be evaluated further, as well as possible grounds for cooperation.

Karl Marx became infamous in his own lifetime for his efforts to bring down the capitalist system and aiming towards the establishment of a socialist take over of the whole world. He lent his name to the ideology of Marxism, which he developed in conjunction with Frederick Engels in order to promote revolutions and bring about the end of capitalism (Hobsbawm, 1987 p. 136). As far as Marx was concerned history was on his side and the working classes of the world would unite and overthrow their capitalist oppressors, Yet socialist revolutions had to be prepared for, with Marx urging his followers to make sure that they were prepared to take opportunities to launch revolutions as soon as these occurred. He was convinced that knowing capitalism inside and out by examining it's strengths and weaknesses would prove invaluable in winning the class war (Marx, 1968 p. 577). In that respect criticising liberal philosophy makes a great deal of sense as that was used to extol the virtues of capitalism. Undermining and attacking liberal philosophy was also a means of weakening support for capitalism itself. Convincing people that liberal philosophy was wrong in it's support of capitalism would end their confidence in the capitalist system (Eatwell & Wright, 2003 p. 31).

For Marx, liberal philosophy could never be trusted because of it's close links to, and it's endorsement of capitalism and the suppression of the working classes. The starting point of the Marxist critique of liberal philosophy was therefore it's unconditional support of, and endorsement of capitalism as the most productive and efficient economic system without regard of how badly the working classes were treated (Marx, 1968 p. 35). The fact that capitalism was more productive than the feudal system it replaced could not be denied, yet it was also more effective at repressing the working classes. Liberal philosophy was an enemy of the working classes as it defended the middle classes and the business owners who gained the most from the dominance of capitalism. Those who agree with liberal philosophy therefore support capitalism and must be considered foes of the working classes. Marx and Engels that their "scientific socialism," would eventually lead to the overthrow of capitalism (Marx 1968 p. 379). If Marxist takeovers could happen peacefully without bloodshed then Anarchist would be more likely to consider joining forces with Marxists to topple the capitalist system (Scott, 2012 x).

Liberal philosophy and it's unconditional justification of capitalism means that all Marxists should aim to wreak it's validity as it condones the alienation of the working classes and the subordinate position of the proletariat. Marx contended that liberal philosophy should be condemned as a tool of capitalist exploitation at every available opportunity. Marxists had to refute that liberal philosophy was the most enlightened or progressive philosophy and that it's sole purpose was as a propaganda tool for capitalism. Marxists had to consistently argue that liberal philosophy and all of it's followers were propping up capitalism and in turn extending the oppression of the working classes and their continued alienation. Condemning liberalism was a key part in preparing the way for revolutions to bring about socialism (Marx 1968 p. 603). Anarchists would consider joining in with such efforts as a means of ending the demeaning aspects of capitalism on the majority of human beings (Scott, 2012 p. 59).

Where Marxist could learn from Anarchism is how to cause agitation and disruption. While Marx thoroughly researched capitalism and it's strengths and faults, he was not particularly an expert in causing chaos. Marx understand propaganda yet the finer points of agitation was not his specialist area. Rightly or wrongly Marx never came up with a blueprir for starting and successfully completing revolutions. What he did do w spend time making sure that socialist parties did not get fooled into accepting concessions from the capitalist state and give up the struggle to achieve socialism by revolutionary means (Marx, 1968 p. 633). His idea of continually condemning liberal philosophy as a pillar of capitalism was basically a good idea for promoting socialism yet witho agitation it could a long time to weaken capitalism unless any severe economic, political, or social crisis took place. He predicted that such a crisis would be caused by imperialism, which he described as "the highest stage of capitalism (Marx 1968 p. 576)."

Anarchism instinctively knew more about agitation than Marxism did, certainly whilst Marx was still alive. Marx himself consider it importar that Marxism showed that it was intellectually superior to liberal philosophy yet later Marxists became concerned about taking power through agitation and also revolutions. That need not stop Lenin pickin an academic or political argument with anybody that disagreed with hi variations of Marxist ideology. However, there were Marxists that proved to be highly effective at causing agitation and using it to undermine a capitalist state, the Bolsheviks in Russia in October 1917. They were given a helping hand by the Germans who put Lenin on a train from Switzerland to Russia (Hobsbawm, 1994 p. 27). In a sense Marx was right that imperialism would cause a severe crisis in capitalism as the First World War caused the collapse of the Austrian, German, Russian and Turkish empires. The Bolsheviks had taken advantage of the collapse of the imperial regime and their propaganda and agitation against the Provisional Government for continuing an imperialist war was highly effective (Harvey, 2003 p. 30).

The October Revolution acted as an example for Marxist parties and indeed Anarchists to prove that they could seize power by revolutionar means if they developed and put into operation revolutionary strategies In the Inter-War period it seemed that further successful revolutionary seizures of power would take place as liberal philosophy and capitalisn found it difficult to readjust themselves after the great trauma of the Fir World War (Marx, 1968 p. 23). The war has devastated the German economy and Russia, while France and Belgium suffered a great deal o physical loss. In theory Britain and France reached the zenith of their respective empires after gaining control of former German and Turkish colonies yet their economies and their morale were damaged severely despite been on the winning side. Yet revolution did not succeed in

Europe outside of the new Soviet Union (Harvey, 2003 p. 50). These were crisis years for liberal philosophy and capitalism, yet Marxism and Anarchism lost out to other alternatives to capitalism especially after the Great Depression. The Fascists in Italy and the National Socialists in Germany both took control as they convinced the king and president respectively that they could end instability and stop Marxism taking over. The price of Fascist and National Socialist regimes taking over was the end of liberal democracy yet capitalism remained intact but harnessed to increasing military power. Germany started the Second World War after signing a Non Aggression Pact with the Soviet Union yet Hitler's bid to destroy communism and Marxism ultimately failed (Hobsbawm, 1994 p. 221).

With Marxism having succeeded in replacing capitalism at least in the Soviet Union that did provide incentives for Anarchists to review what Marxism could offer them in terms of providing tactics for undermining liberal philosophy and capitalism. The concept of alienation was something that lent itself to Anarchism as a means of recruiting members to it's groups and as way of inciting agitation against the injustices and inequalities created and made worse by the capitalist means of ownership and production (Hobsbawm, 1962 p. 160). There was no need for people to endure the alienation that capitalism made worse within societies as it found ever more efficient ways to mass produce goods and services without giving the workers back in return except for low wages and poor working conditions. Workers did not have to sit back and take the poor conditions and the ever increasing sense of alienation they could join in with Anarchist efforts to overthrow the liberal state and end the capitalist system (Scott, 2012 p. 101).

A further thing that Anarchism can learn from Marxism is that is needs to be better organized so that it can resist the and refute the arguments put forward in defending the unequal and restrictive parts of capitalism by liberal philosophy (Tansey, 1995 p. 55). Anarchists should also find ways of demonstrating that liberal philosophy is wrong in extolling the virtues of capitalism. Liberal philosophy falsely provides people with the impression that capitalism and liberal democracy actually provide people with the means to become wealthy and to have complete social and political freedom. Capitalism does not make people free, it makes some people rich and some companies even richer yet it restricts freedom especially for the poor in hidden ways. Liberal philosophy contends that capitalism gives consumers greater freedom than any othe economic system as it is more productive and produces what they want and in the quantities consumers demand. Yet people who cannot afford luxuries and are unable to provide themselves with the basics for survival do not feel free or that the state cares that they even exist. Anarchists can learn from the organization and the propaganda of the Marxists. Marx after all was dismissing the lies that liberal philosophy was peddling about the virtues of capitalism from the 1840s (Marx, 196 p.35). Since then the workers of the world have rarely been united, or when they have been united it has not been for long enough to seriously weaken capitalism. When revolutions have taken place peasants and workers seem to have replaced inept oppressors with more competent whether they called themselves communist or nationalists (Scott, 2012 xi).

Perhaps it is a surprise that Marxism and Anarchism have not cooperate with each other on a continuous basis to weaken liberal philosophy and thus undermine capitalism as well. Supporters of liberal philosophy argue that following their beliefs will make everybody free (Hobsbawn 1962 p. 161). Yet that is not strictly true as capitalism is a system that works on the basis of exploitation. The exact amount of exploitation tha individuals and groups have to suffer depends on their place within the capitalist system. Basically the lower down individuals and groups are the system the greater the amount they are being exploited. Furthermore if the people at the bottom of the social order do not cooperate with eac other then they will feel even more insignificant (Scott, 2012 p. 58). Now capitalism has survived because those that gain the most from it will find ways to divide the opposition to it so that they can divide and continue to rule. The leading capitalists are prepared to improve the wages and the conditions of the most skilled workers to keep them joining forces with everybody else as they are getting more from capitalism than the other workers. Capitalist states are content to provid basic social welfare so that people are not so poor that they will rise up against the system. As soon as people start to rely on the state they will no longer work to change it and to overthrow the capitalist system (Marx, 1968 p. 35).

Marxists and Anarchists should cooperate to refute the propaganda that liberal philosophy provides to support the capitalist system. Supporters of liberal philosophy play down it's role in convincing people how good the capitalist system is to them. Liberals argue that capitalism provides everybody with a higher standard of living, greater personal opportunities, unrestricted human rights, and complete freedom. With

people getting everything they could possibly ask for, or want from capitalism there is no reason for wanting any other kind of economic or political system dominating the world (Scott, 2012).

Supporters of liberal philosophy may have believed that Marxism was no longer a threat to capitalism with the end of the Soviet Union and China's abandonment of communist economics to become the world's largest producer of goods within the capitalist economy (Eatwell & Wright, 2003 p. 280). However that should not be the case as the Soviet Union and China in many respects had never been fully Marxist states. Instead their party leaderships became more interested in holding on to power than achieving true socialism within their borders (Harvey, 2003 p. 295). Indeed now is the time when Marxists and Anarchists should increase their **efforts to discredit liberal** philosophy as it's flaws remain in place and capitalism continues to dominate and exploit all of the individuals and groups who have nothing in the world. They believe that they have real choices yet the poor have less options in capitalist countries than the wealthy do (Scott, 2012 p. 57).

Marxists and Anarchists should use the technological advances that capitalism has provided to demonstrate the harm liberal philosophy continues to do by supporting the capitalist system. Technology and the process of globalization have been presented as evidence of the superiority of capitalism as an economic system (Eatwell & Wright, 2003 p. 282). For those who oppose liberal philosophy the advent of the internet increases the opportunities to combine to act against the capitalist system and to spread the message that there are viable alternatives to liberal democracy and capitalism available. Demonstrations against the G8 / G20 summits and globalization shows that there is support for opposing further capitalist control of the global economy (Klein, 2007 p. 271). Technology increases the scope for people to have autonomy away from the capitalist system and the state to a certain extent. As technology advances even further it should further increase the ability to feel independent of their respective government and free of liberal philosophy and it's blanket endorsement of capitalism (Scott, 2012 p.129).

Liberal philosophy is rightfully criticised by both Marxists and Anarchists as it defends the inequalities that the capitalist system creates and then expands. People should not readily accept it if the capitalist

system leaves them in a considerably worse position than other people. The liberal assertion that all people are considered equal before the law is made null and void by the social and economic inequalities that capitalism worsens. Marx was adamant that workers had to resist the divisive results of capitalism (Marx, 1968 p. 224). Anarchists would certainly protest against how unfair the capitalist system is, and argue that liberal philosophy is deeply flawed as it does not condemn the inequality of capitalism. They would definitely consider joining demonstrations against capitalism in the hope bringing real change (Scott, 2012 p. 32).

Anarchists would carry out revolutionary changes in how they lived to prove that liberal philosophy and capitalism were wrong in how they got people to think and behave. As Anarchists they would set about living revolutionary as it would weaken the state and demonstrate to others that it is possible to live without the state ordering individuals how to act and the capitalist system deciding their place and their value within society. They would not condone the use of violence to bring about revolution (Scott, 2012 p. 102).

On the other hand Marxists would not rule out the use of force to achieve their aims of removing capitalism and liberalism. Marxists are ready to start a revolution at all times as they prepare for the defeat of capitalism (Marx, 1968 p. 576).

Therefore there are things that Marxists and Anarchists hold in common in terms of criticising liberal philosophy and it's unstinting support for the capitalist system. Both would argue that liberal philosophy was flawed because it backed the inequality and the injustices created and worsened by capitalism. Marxism and Anarchism refute the claims that liberalism and capitalism are the best combination for everybody in the world having meaningful and true freedom.

Poverty and inequality for the great majority of the global population means that lives under capitalism and liberalism are only meaningful and good for the richest individuals. Agitation, propaganda and protests are the ways that Marxists and Anarchists can work together to overturn liberal philosophy and capitalism. Revolution and living revolutionary are also ways, in which Marxists and Anarchists could work together to achieve real and lasting change.

It is better that they cooperate with each other to transform the world than it would be struggle against liberal philosophy by themselves and inadvertently allow it to continue fighting to protect and promote capitalism. Without cooperation capitalism will

carry on controlling societies by it's divide and rule strategy. Yet such cooperation rarely takes place and in many places Marxists and Anarchists do not act together to achieve shared objectives. Anarchists tend to be weary that when Marxists have got into positions of power that consolidating power has been given greater priority than increasing levels of freedom.

Bibliography

Eatwell R & Wright A (2003) Contemporary Political Ideologies 2nd edition, Continuum, Stroud

Harvey R (2003) Comrades - The Rise and Fall of World Communism Collins Harper, London

Hobsbawm E (1987) Age of Empire 1875 - 1914, Weidenfeld & Nicholson, London

Hobsbawm E (1994) Age of Extremes: The Short Twentieth Century 1914 - 1991, Michael Joseph, London

Klein N (2007) The Shock Doctrine, Penguin, New York
Marx K (1968) Selected Works in One Volume, Progress Publishers, Moscow

Scott J (2012) Two cheers for Anarchism: Six Easy Pieces on Autonomy, Dignity, and Meaningful Work and Play, Princeton University Press, Princeton

Tansey S D (1995) Politics - The Basics second edition, Routledge, London & New York

In considering the process of change in Russia and the Soviet Union over the whole period 1861 – 1964 how far can the Bolshevik Revolution be seen as the turning point?

This brief evaluation aims to discuss whether or not the most profound changes that affected firstly Imperial Russia and then secondly its successor state the Soviet Union between 1861 and 1964 were most significant during the rule of the Soviet Communist party in general. In particular the assessment will examine the arguments for and against the notion that the Bolshevik Revolution was the main turning point in the changes that took place during this 103 year period. The Imperial Russian government had considered the need to carry out changes in a slow as well as a controlled way. They set out to avoid revolution especially after the revolution of 1905 had forced Nicholas II to concede political concessions but the regime had recovered its composure by the eve of the First World War in 1914.

The Bolsheviks were intent upon bringing about massive changes for the fulfillment of their over all ideological objectives. They aimed to make their own turning points instead of waiting for history to take its natural course. They had followed this ideological notion after it had been developed by their leader Vladimir Lenin. In this respect Lenin had completely reversed the conventional logic of Marxist ideology. Thus in order to bring about the world's very first Marxist / Communist nation state they had to take over the former Russian empire. Or at least as much of it as was possible in the wake of the collapse of the Tsarist regime and the obvious weakness of the Provisional government. The Provisional government had carried on fighting in the war and that had not allowed them to restore stability and reduced their ability to withstand revolution or indeed the German Army (Hobsbawm, 1994 p. 14).

In reality it had been the very frailty of the Provisional government that the had persuaded the leadership of the Bolshevik party to launch the October Revolution in the first place. Lenin and his colleagues regarded the Bolshevik Revolution not only as a turning point for Russia and then the Soviet Union, they believed it was the greatest turning point in world history since the French Revolution. They also assumed that their revolution if it survived would bring about or usher in a worldwide Proletarian victory over feudalism and capitalism. Lenin and his followers were using favourable conditions to bring history forward a century or two early (Lenman, 2004 p. 470).

In theory at least the Communist party were always intent upon bringing extensive economic, political, and social changes upon the land they ruled in the name of the working classes. On the other hand whilst the governments of the last three Tsars were hoping to modernize the very backward Russian empire they only wanted to support the reforms, which strengthened the autocracy instead of adopting policies that would accelerate its demise. These reforms had started the process of changing the Russian empire but in the process inadvertently promoted the growth of underground political parties and also anarchist groups that were determined to remove the monarchy and in some cases end capitalism as well (Roberts, 1996 p. 429).

Both the old Tsarist and the more ideologically focused Bolshevik regimes were determined to bring the massive land area into the modern world at least in terms of economic productivity. The rule of the reform minded Tsar Alexander II started the changes that occurred in the studied era happening, partly through his own desire for economic reform, and because of the weaknesses highlighted during the Crimean War. The Russian economy was largely agrarian and unable to produce enough munitions to sustain a long war against more advanced countries such as Great Britain and France. Although the Russians with large population could replace those killed in action with thousands if not millions of new recruits they found it very difficult to replace spent ammunition and lost weapons.

The main method by which Alexander II and his government sought to alter the Russian empire was via the emancipation of the vast peasant population.

The setting free of the peasantry from their feudal chains without a doubt helped to raise the levels of industrial development throughout the whole of Russia.

However the emancipation of the serfs was not as beneficial as the government had hoped it would be. Further more for the vast bulk of these serfs ended up being poorer instead of actually getting richer. The emancipation of the serfs was therefore not the most profound change or indeed the major turning point that happened in the era. Perhaps if the setting free of the peasants had not taken place at all then it would have made it harder for the Bolsheviks and other revolutionary parties to overthrow the autocracy.

The serfs that remained on the land were more often as not in a poorer situation due to the fact that these poor agrarian workers and their usually large families had to now pay rent to their own landlords. These landowners were amongst the wealthiest people inside the Russian empire. Their peasants had to pay them as well as having to pay taxes to the Russian government. Therefore it was grinding levels of poverty were in many respects just as a much a barrier to Russian peasants been free. Unlike Serfdom poverty was an informal form of enslavement that the state simply did nothing to reduce.

Alexander II's reign was also a period marked by an upsurge in revolutionary activities aimed at weakening or even overthrowing the autocratic Russian monarchy. The growths of revolutionary threats to the autocracy were an unintended consequence of the government's limited economic, political, and social reforms.

Over the short run the draconian security policies of Alexander III had shored up the imperial government. Yet over the long run the repression of all opposition groups including the Bolsheviks in the end raised popular resentment of the Imperial regime. Alexander III made reactionary changes that were intended to prevent revolutionary turning points.

As part of his strategy he thus decided to take away political power away from remote areas of his empire and instead put them it into his own hands in the imperial capital of St Petersburg (Crystal 1998 p. 40). Alexander III had unintentionally made resentment in the border areas of the Russian Empire worse as he had reduced the speaking of non - Russian languages for all official affairs. He had also done his best to spread anti-Semitism across the empire that had terrible results in the violence surrounding the Revolution of 1905. Alexander III had pursued policies that had been designed to prevent change of any kind were to fall apart for the inept Nicholas II, his totally inadequate son. The failings of the last Tsar were instrumental in the autocracy falling apart at the seems in the face of heavy loses on the Eastern Front. A far more capable autocrat might have been able to prevent the Bolshevik Revolution from happening let alone been the turning point of changes in Russia (James., 2003 p. 61).

The Bolsheviks were aiming to enforce as well as actually bring about a wholly socialist economic order to turn the world's largest nation state into a truly communist one. They were to find that this task would be very hard to achieve and that they had a great deal of opposition in their way before the modernization of Soviet Russia was completely finished. However as a consequence of the punitive peace treaty with Germany and the disruption caused by the Russian Civil War the most advanced and therefore the most productive parts of the deceased Tsarist empire were now outside the borders of the newly formed Soviet Union. The first Soviet leader Vladimir Lenin had set out to totally take apart the capitalist economic system in what was left of the former Russian Empire, yet they that had to settle for transforming the areas that they controlled at the end of the Russian Civil War. Revolutionary fervor would to take a back seat until the regime was secure from the most dangerous internal and external threats (Roberts, 1996 p, 405).

The Bolsheviks had promised to nationalize all businesses and farm lands whilst ending Russian involvement in the First World War. After all the

war effort and the dire consequences of defeat had been crucial in fatally undermining the government of the last Tsar. Lenin told Trotsky to stop
involvement in the Great War at any cost to protect the onset of Communism in Russia.

All of the potential advantages, which the future Soviet Communist party could have derive from leaving the fighting on the Eastern Front during the First World War were effectively wiped out by the brutality of the peace terms enforced by the Germans and the onset of the Russian Civil War. At the peak of the Russian Civil War the situation for the Bolsheviks seemed so hopeless that the seriously concerned Lenin brought in the highly draconian policy officially described as War Communism. This harsh policy gave the Red Army enough resources to win the civil war yet ruined the economy.

To temporarily revive the shattered shell of an economy the Bolsheviks introduced the stop gap measure of the New Economic Policy. The NEP for a few years delayed the profound changes that the Communist party was actually committed to achieve over the long -term. What allowed this policy to restore the food supplies and slowly revive production levels was the fact that reduced amounts of state intervention were playing a lesser role thus allowing capitalist elements to return. Allowing a limited form of capitalism to return to restore food stuffs reached the previously starved city dwellers was a pragmatic policy. The problem with the NEP was that it was not a policy that the planners of the Bolshevik Revolution would ever have kept in place. It was designed and then put into place to be a temporary fix to a significant problem. If Lenin had lived it is highly likely that he would have ended it as soon as possible.

The future form of the Soviet economy was an essential area of contention in the contest to find Lenin's successor. As Stalin and his main rival Trotsky sought to gain control of the Soviet Union the NEP continued. Although Stalin protected the NEP it was only as part of his tactics to force Trotsky into foreign exile.

He then borrowed his rival's strategy to collectivize agriculture hand in hand with policies to industrialize. It was under the brutal guidance of Joseph Stalin that the Bolshevik Revolution and the resultant Soviet regime introduced the most radical changes endured between 1861 and 1964. For it was the highly neurotic Stalin who ruthlessly carried out his modernization and development policies to wipe out all political opposition within rural areas, especially the detested Kulaks.

The wiping out of the Kulaks was not only vicious, it was also short sighted. It was short sighted as the Kulaks were the most productive farmers and agricultural workers within the Soviet Union itself. Yet they were detested by Stalin due to the fact that they were richer peasants that got extra money due to their abilities to grow food more effectively than the majority of the other peasants .

The Soviet leadership's official war against the Kulaks was very damaging to the Soviet economy over the long term although Stalin carried on with it in order to destroy all of the opposition to his misguided rule. Stalin without a doubt dragged one of the world's most backward economies into the modern era but a terrible human cost. The bloody minded way in which he did so meant that the NKVD, famine, and also disease would go on to kill tens of millions of the Soviet Union's economically and agriculturally most effective people in the twin processes of collectivization and industrialization. These were momentous changes but they were also the central features of a highly flawed Communist command economy. It would contribute to the weaknesses of a system that crack with the cost of the renewed nuclear arms of the 1980s and the inadequate technological advance of the economy (Woodruff. 2005 p. 199).

Bibliography

Crystal, D. - The Cambridge Biographical Encyclopedia 2nd edition (1998) Cambridge

Hobsbawm, E *Age of Extremes the Short Twentieth Century 1914-1991*, (1994) Michael Joseph, London

Lenman B, (2004) Chambers Dictionary of World History, Edinburgh

James H, (2003) Europe Reborn – A History, 1914 – 2000, Pearson Longman, Harlow

Palmowski J, (2008) Oxford Dictionary of Contemporary World History, Oxford

Roberts J.M, (1996) A History of Europe, Penguin, London

Woodruff W, *A Concise History of the Modern World*, (2005) Abacus, London

The continuities in the Soviet relationship with East Germany (1945-1989)

East Germany was created as a result of the circumstances surrounding the defeat of Nazi Germany and the onset of the Cold War between the Soviet Union and the United States plus their respective allies and satellite states. The post-war partition of Germany between the four powers decided at the Yalta and Potsdam conferences had only meant to be temporary, to prevent any resurgence of German military power. Germany was supposed to have been reunited after the completion of denazification and demilitarisation programmes. With the Cold War though the three zones controlled by Britain, France and the United States were merged to form West Germany in 1949 with the Soviet Union duly responding by turning its zone into East Germany later that year (Bullock, 1991, p1026). As will be discussed below various continuities could be observed in the relationship between the Soviet Union and East Germany in the forty-five years between 1945 and 1989.

The first continuity that can be seen between the Soviet Union and East Germany was the leading role of the Communist Party in both countries. Occupation by the Red Army meant that Stalin could impose single Communist Party rule on East Germany as it was maintained in the Soviet Union. The Communist party (KPD) and the Social Democrats (SPD) in East Germany were merged to form the SED or Socialist Unity Party that became the leading party if not the sole party in East Germany. Other parties were allowed but their independence from the regime and their positions within parliament were purely nominal. The merger between the KPD and SPD had occurred to ensure the Communists could win elections prior to them taking over the government of the Soviet zone (Fullbrook, 1991, p.136). Walter Ulbrecht was a devoted Stalinist and was keen to toe the Moscow line. He became the SED leader who gladly imposed the Stalinist version of Marxist-Leninism on East Germany.

East Germany was counted, as one of the countries of 'really existing socialism' or a Peoples democracy along with the Soviet Union's other Central and East European satellites. Communist rule was legitimised by claiming the leading role of the Communists would eventually over take capitalism and provided socialist utopias (Hobsbawm, 1994, p.373). The government of East Germany were also sure that the Red Army would help to maintain communist rule at gunpoint if needs be. The Soviets believed that a communist East Germany was in their best interests, the SED regime in turn looked to the Soviet Union (Roberts, 1999, p.513). The adoption of communism in East Germany was meant to show a greater break from Nazism than was the case in West Germany as all those capitalist that had co-operated with the Nazis regime lost their economic and political

influence in the East. For the Soviets it would have been unacceptable that East Germany could be allowed to be a capital liberal democracy. Communism was the strongest cause of continuity between the Soviets and East Germany (Pulzer, 1995, p.7).

A continuity in the relationship between the Soviets and East Germany was the insistence that unless it came about on their terms Germany reunification would not happen at all. The Soviet Union saw the maintenance of East Germany as vital to the success and continuance of the Warsaw Pact and its hegemony over Central and Eastern Europe. The ruling SED in East Germany realised that reunification on West Germany's terms would lead to East Germany being absorbed into West Germany and the very real prospect of their regime being removed. When the Soviets did offer the chance of reunification it was on terms unacceptable to West Germany and her allies. Both the Soviet Union and the East German regime saw the continuance of two German states better than the prospect of a united Germany firmly in the Western camp. At the council of Foreign Ministers in May 1949 held in Paris the four powers were not prepared to compromise to achieve reunification (Bullock, 1991, p.1034). For as long as there was a Cold War the Soviet and East German regimes needed each other.

The division of Germany was allowed continue to maintain the balance between the superpowers. As soon as the Soviet Union ended the Cold War it meant East Germany no longer had a viable future. For that meant that the Soviets were no longer prepared to use its armed forces to prop up the hard line East German regime of Eric Honecker (Hobsbawm, 1994, p.252).

For much of the period 1945 to 1989 the Soviet Union's relationship with East Germany was closely bound to the formal, military, political and economic links operated through the Warsaw Pact and COMECON (the Council for Mutual Economic Aid). The Warsaw Pact was established during May 1955 in response to NATO allowing West Germany to join it and re-arm. East Germany had its own separate Soviet equipped armed forces by the end of 1956. The East German military complimented the Soviet forces already on East German soil. As well as being used to counter the threat from NATO it was used for internal security duties within East Germany. The East German army was important for the continuance of the Soviet-East German army relationship as it supported the East German regime and worked closely with the Soviet forces in East Germany (Watson, 1997, p.89). The East Berlin uprising and unrest throughout the rest of East Germany had been put down by the Soviets. The East Germans may have taken over internal security duties yet it and the East German regime survived due to the presence of the Soviet's garrisons and the guarantee that they would be used to keep the SED in power (Watson, 1997, pp.170-71). Added to this was the National People's Army around

200,000 strong that tried to prevent its fellow east Germans crossing the border and later the Berlin Wall into the West (Fullbrook, 1991, p.180). As the East German regime was officially anti-Fascist and anti-capitalist it naturally led to a continuance of the political, military and economic relationship with the Soviet Union, as it was the world's most obviously anti-Fascist and anti-capitalist state (Pulzer, 1995, p. 9). A further continuance that can be seen in the relationship between the Soviet and East Germany was in the area of economics.

The Soviet Union had been driven by two aims in East Germany, to gain economic reparations and to make the East German economy a command economy. The soviets gained an estimated $30 billion from East Germany in the decade after 1945. The economy of the Soviet zone was well on the way to being turn into a Stalinist style command economy prior to the formal emergence on East Germany in 1949. Most private land estates and businesses were taken into state control on the grounds that they were owned by pro-Nazi's landowners and industrialists. Private sector businesses and industries had already been forced, cajoled and taxed into becoming state controlled by 1955. The imposition of state controlled socialism was viewed as elementary to the foundation and maintenance of East Germany plus its relationship with the Soviet Union (Fullbrook, 1991, p.154-55). The Soviet Union had decided to integrate East Germany economically with itself and the others people's Republics of Central and Eastern Europe as part of COMECON in 1952. Officially, COMECON would direct economic development and trade between its members until 1989 (Fullbrook, 1991, p.179).

Therefore, the continuities that can be seen in the Soviet relationship with East Germany included the leading role of the Communist Party in countries, the CPSU and SED respectively. Ultimately, the viability of the East German State was heavily dependent on the strength of the Soviet Union plus the continuance of both the communist controls of the Soviet Union and the Cold War between the East and the West. East Germany was the frontline border between East and West. It was thus vital for Soviet interests that its regime was communist and pro-Soviet. Soviet military presence ensured that uprisings like those of 1953 would fail. East Germany was re-armed to make the Warsaw Pact stronger and also integrated into COMECON. The East German regime had to maintain strong links with the Soviet Union because without them it could not survive. The flight of East Germans to West Germany was as big a threat as rebellion. The Berlin Wall for a time stemmed the flow. The Soviets were happy to see East Germany use repressive measures as they used similar methods themselves.

The Soviets rather than the East Germans in fact ended the continuities of the Soviet Union's relationship with East Germany. It was the political reforms of Gorbachev that ended the Cold War and meant that the Soviet Union was no longer willing to impose communism on any of the satellite states of central and Eastern Europe. Once this happened the Honecker regime was moribund and unable to prevent immigration to West Germany and its own replacement.

Bibliography

Fullbrook, M (1991) The Fontana History of Germany –
Germany 1918-1990 the Divided Nation, Fontana, London
Hobsbawm, E (1994) Age of Extremes, the Short Twentieth
Century 1914-1991, Michael Joseph, London
Pulzer, P (1995) German Politics 1945 – 1995, Oxford
University Press, Oxford
Roberts, J M (1996) a History of Europe, Penguin Books,
London
Watson, J (1997) Success in World History since 1945,
John Murray, London

The causes of the Soviet Union's Demise

Was the Soviet Union on its last legs by the mid-1980's or did Gorbachev's policies effectively cause it to implode? That is a question (including different variations of the wording) that has been asked over and over again since the end of the Soviet Union

Outlined below is a discussion as to whether the Soviet Union was indeed on its last legs by the mid 1980s as some have argued. Or if another opinion, which, contends that it, was the policies of the last reforming General Secretary, Mikhail Gorbachev that inadvertently caused the Soviet Union to implode by the end of December 1991 is a more accurate depiction of the causes of that startling disintegration. The Soviet Union collapsed in a relatively short space of time, causing there to be much subsequent debate as to whether it was long-term or short-term factors that contributed the most to such a rapid collapse. If such a spectacular collapse or implosion was avoidable was another feature of the debate, had Gorbachev decided to carry out different policies he may or may not have been able to revive the Soviet Union rather than unwittingly presiding over its demise. Gorbachev will certainly leave a mixed legacy to history, as an individual that contributed to the ending of the Cold War whilst at the same being unable to transform the Soviet Union away from its communist past to a democratic future.

There is certainly plenty of good cause for arguing that the Soviet Union was indeed on its last legs by the mid 1980s when Mikhail Gorbachev came to power as General Secretary. The Soviet Union had been weakened by long term trends that had contributed to increasing levels of economic stagnation, political paralysis in key decision making, as well as high levels of corruption, and increasing signs of potentially separatist nationalism at the individual republic level (Rayner & Stanley, 2006, p.330). By the mid 1980s the Stalinist era economic planning and one party political systems of the Soviet Union were beginning to show their age and their propensity for economic failure, administrative inefficiency, and declining political legitimacy (White, 1990).

The main economic and political institutions as well as it systems dated back to the infrastructure constructed by Stalin in the late1920s and the 1930s. The collectivisation of agriculture and industrialisation had been achieved at great human cost, with political obedience and loyalty to the Communists counting for more than efficiency or ability to do their jobs. The Soviet Union had suffered horrendous losses during the Second World War which were partially compensated by the gaining of satellite states in Central and Eastern Europe (Gaddis, 2005, p.11). The Soviet Union had gained superpower status by the end of the Second World War, which led to the emergence to the Cold War.

However, the financial costs of funding Soviet military strength during the Cold War played a significant role in the Soviet Union being on its last legs by the mid 1980s. Despite these weakness its hold on the Central and Eastern European states in military terms was still secure up to the mid 1980s and beyond (Ferguson, 2007, p.625).

For the Soviet Union the strain of maintaining its military bases in Central and Eastern Europe was a bearable cost of its superpower status in political terms, especially as the Soviet Army had been protecting the Soviet Union's strategic interests for the previous four decades by been there. Most importantly previous Soviet leaders had not tolerated dissidence internally or any signs of autonomy from its satellite states in Central and Eastern Europe. For instance the crushing of the Hungarian revolt in 1956 and the invasion of Czechoslovakia in 1968. However the willingness of the Soviet leadership to keep its forces in Central and Eastern Europe ignored the rising economic strain of keeping soldiers based there. Two factors related to the increasing costs of the military industrial complexes and actual weapons acquirement arguably played roles in putting the Soviet Union on to its last legs by the mid 1980s. Firstly the Soviet Union had decided to invade Afghanistan during 1979 to prop up the communist regime there. As far as the General Secretary Leonid Brezhnev had been concerned there had been sound military and strategic reasons for the Soviet Union intervening in Afghanistan. Brezhnev believed in supporting a reliable client regime.

At the time it was also resisting the risk of Islamic fundamentalism that could have spread to Soviet republics like Kazakhstan and Uzbekistan with sizeable Muslim populations (Judt, 2007, p.593). The Soviets decision to invade Afghanistan effectively ended the détente with the United States and thus prompted the second factor, a renewed superpower arms race that severely tested the Soviet economy. For the United States, the Soviet invasion of Afghanistan presented the ideal opportunity for the Soviet Union to become embroiled in a long lasting conflict which placed increasing strain upon the Soviet economy and sapped away the confidence of the Soviet regime. It started out, as a short-term military intervention, but soon became an expensive stay for a decade (Hobsbawm, 1994 p. 479) Perhaps if the Soviet economy been in a better shape it might have been able to have matched the American increase in military expenditure without damaging itself even further (James, 2003, p.371).

The section of the Soviet economy dedicated to military research and production, unlike the rest of the economy, remained in working order (Hobsbawm, 1994, p.476). The bulk of the Soviet economy remained backward and unproductive (White, 1990). The Soviet agricultural system seemed to be a particularly weak link in the chain as the Soviet Union moved towards being on its last legs. After all as one of the greatest superpowers its agricultural production was so low that it had to import grain from the United States and Western Europe to feed its population (Ferguson, 2007, p.635).

It could also be argued that the Soviet Union was on its last legs by the mid 1980s as the unity of the Soviet state was being undermined by growing levels of nationalism amongst the individual Soviet republics. Nationalism was stronger in some republics; most notably those countries that had previously been independent, than it was in other component republics that had no experience of being fully independent states. On its own nationalism was probably not enough to bring about the end of the Soviet Union, yet in combination with other factors it contributed to putting the Soviet Union on its last legs by the mid 1980s. The Soviet authorities were certainly aware of the possibility of nationalism being capable of breaking up the Soviet Union.

The Communist Party of the Soviet Union itself was the main unifying factor within the Soviet Union. Thus by the mid 1980s some of its members believed that the Soviet Union was in such a poor state that its leadership had the stark choice of leaving things unchanged until stagnation finally finished off the Soviet state. Alternatively, the Soviet Union could be reformed to get off its last legs and revive its fortunes (Hobsbawm, 1994, p.476).

The Soviet Union was visibly in a very poor state by the mid 1980s which certainly seemed to mean that it was on its last legs. The poor condition of the Soviet Union was largely down to the shortcomings of the Communist Party itself. During the last years of the Brezhnev era the corruption and inertia within the Communist party seemed to get in the way of attempts to end the worrying and profound economic stagnation that was weakening the very fabric of the Soviet state drastically (Judt, 2007, p.581). Brezhnev had not seen any reason to end the corruption that lined his own pocket and those pockets of the people closest to him. By the mid 1980s corruption within the Soviet Union was generally considered to be rife, and it was arguably debilitating to the health of the Soviet state (Hobsbawm, 1994 p. 476). General Secretary Andropov might have provided more dynamic leadership if he had not already been terminally ill when he succeeded Brezhnev during 1982. Andropov's successor Chernenko was equally as ancient and only managed to stay in power just as briefly. The old and decrepit nature of the Soviet leadership was not a good omen for the future, although it ultimately allowed Gorbachev to gain power (Judt, 2007, p.594).

There are some convincing counter arguments that the Soviet Union was not actually on its last legs in the 1980s when Gorbachev came to power. The starting point for all those counter arguments was that it was the political, social, and economic policies of Gorbachev that essentially caused the Soviet Union to implode (White, 2000; Hobsbawm, 1994, p.475). There was no denying that the Soviet Union was in a very unhealthy condition by the time of the death of Chernenko. However that did not mean that the Soviet state would inevitably collapse (Ferguson, 2007, 637).

Political, social and economic reforms were not new to the Soviet Union. Lenin had for instance introduced the New Economic Policy in the early 1920s that had allowed limited capitalist activity to revive the Soviet agricultural sector and let it recover from the grave losses of the First World War and the Russian Civil War (Pipes, 2001, p.49). It had been Stalin that had decided the basic political, social and economic structure of the Soviet Union, his successors may have decreased the level of political repression, yet its economic system still remained intact if not still in full working order (Judt, 2007, p.593). Gorbachev could have just attempted to have implemented economic reforms and kept the political structures of the Soviet Union unreformed, as the Chinese had done after the death Mao Zedong. China has enjoyed high economic growth since with its communist regime still in charge. The Soviet regime could have introduced as much or as little capitalist economic reforms and repressed any increased levels of political opposition. Instead Gorbachev decided to introduce a full range of political, social and economic reforms under the slogan of restructuring (Perestroika) and openness (glasnost). No Soviet leader had attempted to carry out so many reforms simultaneously, and with it was a gamble with so much riding on the successful outcome of these measures (Evans & Newnham, 1998, p.207).

The attempts of Gorbachev to reform the Soviet Union would end in disaster due to the way in which the reforms were implemented. Gorbachev and his politburo colleagues regarded reform of the Soviet economy as their main priority. After all they reasoned that if they could not salvage the economy they would not be able to salvage the Soviet Union, as it would be too weak to continue as a superpower, and perhaps even as a state (Hobsbawm, 1994, p.475). Gorbachev decided that the best way to fund economic reform was to drastically reduce the Soviet Union's military involvement abroad, by deciding to withdraw Soviet forces from Central and Eastern Europe as well as effectively ending the Cold War with the United States (Evans & Newnham, 1998, p.207). The Soviet Union effectively gave away its dominance of Central and Eastern Europe to save a few billion roubles.

The ease with which Gorbachev allowed Central and Eastern Europe to go its own way was an indication that his regime had lost its belief in the legitimacy of Marxist ideology. The collapse of the communist regimes in Central and Eastern Europe convinced nationalists in some of the Soviet republics that independence was obtainable, and they that might be able to achieve it peacefully. They believed that was increasingly likely as Gorbachev seemed to lack the will or nerve to use violence to maintain the territorial integrity of the Soviet Union (Pipes, 2001, p.88).

The policies of Gorbachev led to the implosion of the Soviet Union because his regime gave up the rule of one party communist state and was not able to find an alternative method of achieving political legitimacy with increasing numbers of ordinary people within the Soviet Union itself. Gorbachev was often caught out by his own indecisiveness. Basically he could not decide whether to wholeheartedly back radical reform or to stop the reform process and consolidate his hold on power. The problem for Gorbachev was that whilst he was being indecisive the Soviet Union continued to head toward terminal economic decline and ever increasing levels of political powerlessness (Hobsbawm, 1994, p.478). Had Gorbachev decided to fully reverse his reform policies the Soviet Union still possessed enough military and security services to repress opposition and prevent the break away of separatist republics like Estonia, Latvia and Lithuania. The KGB still had 480,000 staff to repress and detain dissident elements of the population, whilst the Soviet Army still had millions of soldiers available to deal with secessionist republics and opposition movements had Gorbachev wanted to use them (Pipes, 2001, p.85).

Gorbachev's policies inadvertently led to the implosion of the Soviet Union as his regime lost control of the political, economic and social situation within the country allowing the centrifugal forces within the Soviet Union to combine with devastating effect to bring about the final collapse (Ferguson, 2007, p.637). The gathering pace of political and economic disintegration within the Soviet Union alarmed many whilst it was regarded as presenting an opportunity for independence and greater levels of both national and individual freedoms in other quarters.

Soviet republics such as Armenia, Estonia, Lithuania, and Latvia believed that they needed to make the most of their opportunity to leave the Soviet Union, just in case Gorbachev decided to reverse his reforms in order to preserve the Soviet Union. It had to be remembered after all that Gorbachev still had the military capacity to do so by force if political reasoning failed to gain compliance. There was also a doubt for the nationalists in these republics that Gorbachev could remain in power. There were many rumours about there being a strong possibility that their hopes for secession would be ruined if Communist party hard liners removed Gorbachev from power by taking power themselves through a coup backed by the Soviet military and the KGB (Pipes, 2001 p. 89).

Other Soviet republics had been less concerned about gaining independence from the Soviet Union for reasons of nationalism began to reconsider their options as the Soviet Union's economic system started to disintegrate and Gorbachev's political authority was declining rapidly. The communist leaderships of republics such as Kazakhstan, Uzbekistan, and Tajikistan were originally content to remain within the Soviet Union yet changed their minds.

These party leaderships decided that their best hope in an uncertain future was to preserve what remained of the Soviet economic system within their republics. They then decided to reinvent themselves as nationalist leaders and contrived to lead their countries to independence as the best method of keeping hold of their own positions (Hobsbawm, 1994 p. 478).

Gorbachev might have got away with his policies failing to achieve political, social, and economic reforms had he maintained the support of the two largest republics within the Soviet Union, the Russian Federation, and the Ukraine. By 1991 both these republics had presidents willing to go towards independence, Boris Yeltsin, and Leonid Kravchuk respectively. Yeltsin in particular did not like Gorbachev and had heavily criticised him for not introducing reforms quickly enough, the formers election to the Russian Presidency had been a protest against Gorbachev by the Russian voters (James, 2003 p. 382).

Gorbachev's position clearly became untenable during the course of 1991.

As the Soviet republics had either already declared independence or were intending to do so, whilst the economy went from bad to absolutely catastrophic. Gorbachev had already been abandoned by the majority of reformers, and finally Soviet hard liners decided to launch a coup to overthrow him and save the Soviet Union before it was too late (Hobsbawm, 1994 p. 478). The attempted hard line Communist coup of August 1991 will probably go down in history as the one of the most ineptly executed coups ever attempted. The fact that the coup took place at all showed that Gorbachev's policies had completely failed to salvage the Soviet Union. The coup's failure was due to the courage of Boris Yeltsin and thousands of ordinary Russians that took to the streets, combined with the refusal of the army units involved to obey the orders of the coup leaders. Once the coup had failed the disintegration of the Soviet Union was inevitable and no longer avoidable. Gorbachev held an office that was completely meaningless, as all the power had passed to the heads of the Soviet republics, especially Yeltsin and Kravchuk. It was Yeltsin that formally ended the Soviet Union in December 1991, the ultimate demonstration of the failure of Gorbachev's policies (James, 2003 p. 383).

Thus it can be concluded that the policies of Mikhail Gorbachev were inadvertently the most decisive factor in the break up or implosion of the Soviet Union in December 1991. That it is not to deny the importance of the long-term weaknesses that were undermining the effectiveness and the future of the Soviet Union in the mid 1980s when Mikhail Gorbachev became General Secretary of the Soviet Communist party. Gorbachev gained power believing that wide-ranging political, social, and economic reforms were urgently needed to modernise and revitalise the Soviet Union, to reverse economic stagnation, administrative corruption, and political apathy.

Reforms were considered precisely because Gorbachev appreciated that the Soviet Union had long-term problems that needed to be resolved if possible, and as quickly as possible. The long-term problems weakened the Soviet Union yet by themselves did not mean that the Soviet Union was actually on its last legs during the mid 1980s.

Economic stagnation, administrative corruption, a strong sense of nationalism in some of the republics, as well as massive over commitments of resources to the Cold War rivalry with the United States were certainly serious problems, yet at the time did not seem to be fatal problems. Perhaps Gorbachev's main mistake was that he did not stick to an over all strategy for the achievement of his projected political, economic, and social changes. Gorbachev and his advisors also seem to have under estimated the true state of the Soviet economy as their economic reforms proved to be inadequate for the task of reviving economic growth. Instead the economic reforms that were introduced inadvertently speeded up the disintegration of the Soviet economic system. Gorbachev's decision to drastically cut down military spending was probably sensible in the long -term yet the ending of the Cold War, and the peaceful acceptance of the end of communism in Central and Eastern Europe strengthened nationalist movements within the individual Soviet republics. Although nationalist movements had been present before Gorbachev began his reform policies, the Soviet Union had previously avoided any of the republics gaining independence. The knowledge that Gorbachev would not use force to keep republics within the Soviet Union ultimately led to the implosion of the Soviet Union.

Bibliography

Gaddis J L, (2005) The Cold War, Penguin, London
Hobsbawm, E (1994) Age of Extremes, the Short Twentieth
Century 1914-1991, Michael Joseph, London

James H, (2003) Europe Reborn – A History, 1914 – 2000,
Pearson Longman, Harlow

Rayner E, & Stapley R, (2006) History Debunked, Sutton
Publishing, Stroud
White S, (1990) Gorbachev in power, Cambridge
University Press, Cambridge

The relationship between the May 4th Movement, the New Culture Movement and the Chinese Communist Party and assess the impact of this relationship on China's modernisation

Stalin's death in 1953 was Mao's liberation. For more than thirty years Mao had to play supplicant to the leader of the communist world.
(Dikotter, 2010 p,3)

Political power comes from the barrel of a gun
Mao (Fraser, 1990, p. 174)

The following is a description and analysis of the relationship between the May 4th Movement, the New Culture Movement and the Chinese Communist Party (CCP) and how that relationship has contributed to the modernisation of China. Together these movements aimed at the overhaul and modernisation of China for reasons that will be discussed and outlined below. China started the 20th Century backward and weak. That weakness left her prone to foreign interference and intervention not only from Western powers but also from the one modern Asian country during that era, Japan. Japan would be one model of how China could be modernised yet after the 1917 revolution the Soviet Union showed that a communist option was available (Hobsbawm, 1994, p.65). China like Russia seemed an unlikely place for either revolution or modernisation. China had even fewer workers than Russia yet with even more peasants. Under the leadership of Mao Tse-tung the CCP managed to turn the peasantry towards revolution and modernisation. Mao would dominate the relationship between the CCP and the other movements especially after taking power in 1949 (Evans & Newnham, 1998, p.314).

The path towards modernisation in China was far from straight forward. At the start of the 20th Century many blamed China's weaknesses and backwardness on the ailing Imperial dynasty. The dynasty fell in 1911 creating a power vacuum in which the nationalist Kuomintang competed with regional warlords and the CCP formed in 1921 to fill (Tuner, 2000, p.38).

The disarray that China fell into came as a great disappointment to the man who worked hardest for a modern Chinese republic, Sun Yat-sen. Sun Yat-sen was a founding member and the first leader of the Kuomintang that would govern China for much of the period up to 1949. Like the CCP the Kuomintang had a relationship with the May 4th Movement if not the New Culture Movement. The Kuomintang was a nationalist organisation as well, split into capitalist and socialist if not communist factions. On a more practical level Sun Yat-sen helped the process of modernisation by developing China's inadequate train network (Wakin, 1997, p.12).

Many Chinese people deeply resented foreign power and influence in China, which their governments Imperial and Republican were both incapable and unwilling to end. Germany's defeat in the First World War did not lead to the Chinese government taking back German rights in China. Instead of that happening the Allies gave all Germany's rights to the Japanese without bothering to consult the Chinese government. There was mass protest in China leading to the formation of the May 4th Movement. The May 4th Movement was dominated by young Chinese intelligentsia, some of which would later have links with the CCP. Mao himself would be close to some members of the May 4th Movement although his ideas on modernisation and revolution would prove more radical. There were also people in China that wished to radically alter society and culture, the New Culture Movement (Starr, 2001, p.211). The May 4th movement failed in its original aim of returning the city of Qingdao under Chinese control rather than allowing the Japanese to take control of it under the terms of the Versailles Peace Settlement (Wasserstrom, 2003, p.94). The May 4th Movement had an influence both on the Kuomintang and the CCP that tinged both parties with strong nationalist traits yet with differing ideas of modernisation (Wasserstrom, 2003, p.138). For a time it seemed that the Kuomintang and the CCP would work together to modernise China.

Such an alliance seemed practical as both parties claimed to be nationalist and revolutionary whilst looking towards the Soviet Union for support in their struggles against foreign imperialists and backwardness. Things did not turn out that way largely due to the Kuomintang turning on their communist allies once they had tightened their control over the country. Chiang Kai-shek viewed the elimination of the CCP as vital for undisputed control of China as well destroying its links with the May 4th Movement and the New Cultural Movement. Chiang would put destroying them ahead of fighting the Japanese whilst attempting to modernise China. Chiang however was unable to those links and the relationship between the CCP and May 4th Movement and the New Culture Movement (Hobsbawm, 1994, p.70).

Chiang's efforts to modernise China would be hampered by increasing Japanese aggression and invasion of China during the 1930s. These failures would help the CCP build stronger relationships with those from the May 4th Movement and the New Culture Movement that might have followed the Kuomintang instead. Despite his best efforts Chiang could not completely destroy the CCP and the inspirational Mao. It was Mao that allowed the CCP to dominate its relationship with the May 4th Movement and the New Culture Movement. Chiang hoped to modernise China by extending education provision, developing or extending communications whilst attempting to industrialise the country. Chiang also attempted to

modernise the Chinese army although it proved no match against the Japanese even after advice from the German army. The 'New Life Movement' set up in 1934 was intended to shore up the Kuomintang regimes popularity whilst helping to modernise China by persuading people that hard work and morality would lead to national regeneration. The main problem for the New Life Movement was that although Chiang himself was seen as honest, it was a virtue that many of his colleagues in the Kuomintang lacked. In fact the regime's reputation for corruption and greed was as bad as under its Imperial predecessors (Brendon, 2000, p.549).

The New Life movement showed that Chiang and the Kuomintang were aware of the need to have strong nationalist support backing the regime rather than opposed to it. The Kuomintang intended to prove they were the real successors to the nationalist mantle of the May 4th Movement or the social aims of the New Culture Movement rather than the CCP. The claims of the Kuomintang to be the truest Chinese nationalists, the best guardians of Chinese culture and the best people to modernise China would be severely dented by the failure to repel the Japanese invaders. Chinese resistance to the Japanese was sporadic, strong in places yet inept or non-existent in other places. Even if the Kuomintang had not been distracted by its campaigns against the CCP they were militarily no where near a match for the better -trained and equipped Japanese. The West looked on whilst the Japanese did what they wanted whilst military supplies from the Soviet Union were not enough to equip either government forces or the communists (Brendon, 2000, p.547). For the most part Mao and the Red Army avoided pitched battles with either Kuomintang forces or the Japanese invaders. Mao had learnt the hard way that his Red Army was at that stage no match for Chiang in a pitched battle. Defeated in 1934 Mao and his followers embarked on the long March during October 1934. Mao in the areas that the Chinese Communist Party controlled would show to many Chinese that lived in government controlled areas that the best hopes for food and land as well as modernising China lay with him. All the trials and tribulations of the CCP meant that many Chinese believed it had earned the right to take over the mantles of the May 4th Movement and the New Culture Movement (Wakin, 1997, pp.28-29).

Unlike Lenin and Trotsky in 1917 Mao did not have any working class militant proletariat to help him seize power even if he wanted to use them because there were none to speak of. Mao had grasped quickly that the key to political power plus social, economic and eventually a Cultural Revolution and modernisation was gaining the support of the hundreds of millions of the Chinese peasantry.

Failure to gain this support had restricted the success of the May 4th Movement and later the New Culture Movement. In that respect the relationship between the CCP and the May 4th Movement and the New Culture Movement was based on the CCP examining the successes and failures of the two movements. If Mao could use the support of the peasants instead of Chiang he could chose how China would be modernised. Although Mao was a committed Marxist he adapted Marxist doctrines to fit Chinese conditions. Not only did he base the revolutionary tactics of the CCP around inciting the peasants rather than the workers towards revolution he maintained that political will was of greater importance than social and economic conditions or progress. Mao saw China's biggest failure to modernise politically, economically and socially as been due to her exploitation by the West and Japan. In other words Mao was more than happy to associate the CCP with Chinese nationalism and the cultural greatness of the Chinese combined with the wasted potential of the peasants. Mao and the CCP intended to fulfil their own aims, yet those aims shared some from the May 4th Movement and the new Culture Movement. While the CCP went down the path of creating a strong established communist state these aims were seen as compatible with modernising China and making her resistant to foreign intervention or exploitation. Whilst at the same time sweeping away the social, economic and cultural elite that had prospered even as the country languished in its backwardness (Eatwell and Wright, 2003, p. 119).

For Mao gaining the support of the peasants paid dividends during the fighting against the Kuomintang and the Japanese. The support of the peasants not only allowed the Chinese Communist Party to gain power it also meant that it became far more powerful than any of the other movements that wished to modernise China. To win the war against the Japanese and the civil war against Chiang and the Kuomintang government, Mao with the Red Army mainly drawn from the peasantry fought long term guerrilla campaigns.

The CCP gained in popularity as it stressed the relationship between its ideas and those of the May 4th Movement and the New Culture Movement. The other thing that Mao was to develop was an effective civil service wherever the Chinese Communist Party gained control. Mao contended that it would be impossible to control China let alone modernise without the Red Army or a civil service (Hobsbawm, 1994, p.79).

In many ways Mao was like his mentor, Joseph Stalin in that he was from a peasant background and used the support of the peasantry (admittedly in different circumstances). Mao like Joseph Stalin believed that the best hope for his country's success was rapid modernisation no matter what the human and environmental costs. As with Stalin Mao was prepared to sacrifice millions of lives to fulfil his own aim of bringing China into the modern world. Just because Mao understood the peasants did not mean that he was not prepared to sacrifice their lives. This was were the relationship between the May 4th Movement had been weakest as it had not concentrated on the peasantry for support or wished to sacrifice them. Mao would allow up to 20 million of his own people to starve to death, a scale of famine previously only seen in the Soviet Union during the early 1930s. In some ways it could be argued that the relationship between the CCP and the CPSU was more important than with the May 4th Movement and the New Culture Movement (Brendon, 2000, p. 211).

Alongside the economic and industrial modernisation of China, Mao of course instigated a Cult of Personality and indoctrination of the Chinese people with Marxism. The Cult of Personality worked not only because of well -used propaganda, it gained momentum from Mao's reputation of standing up for China and its people. Mao and the Red Army had resisted the Japanese and went on to defeat Chiang who had placed greed and corruption ahead of ruling the country.

Mao was popular with the majority of the Chinese people. For the vast majority of the peasantry their standard of living improved markedly in the first decade of the CCP's rule. While many benefited from the distribution of land to the landless peasants all opponents of the regime were brutally repressed. The relationship with the New Culture Movement was stronger here as the CCP altered culture and society by breaking up the old elite although inadvertently created new ones (Wakin, 1997, p.31). The CCP had gained power due to being well organised, the willingness to exploit nationalism within the peasantry and the promise of radical social and economic modernisation. The Chinese supported the CCP as it promised them a much better future and made the present much improved from the past (Wasserstrom, 2003, p.143).

Mao himself was not happy with the pace or direction of China's modernisation which prompted him to launch two major campaigns to alter China economically and culturally, The Great Leap Forward of 1958 – 60 plus the later Cultural Revolution started in 1966 (Turner, 2000,p.61).

The New Culture Movement was to be closely associated with the Cultural Revolution that was the direct result of the CCP attempting to make the increasing number of workers the cultural epicentre of China and attempts to modernise her. The New Culture Movement had originally started in the 1920s and its main influence upon the CCP was the concept that a uniform of culture could be imposed upon the whole of the Chinese people. For Mao the best culture that could be imposed upon China was that of the working class proletariat as opposed to either that of the peasant or the intellectualism of the CCP bureaucrats or factory technicians (Wasserstrom, 2003, pp. 232-33).

The Great Leap Forward had been a direct result of Mao allowing people to criticise the government in public in the 1957 'Hundred Flowers Campaign'. The Chinese Communist Party had expected little criticism and

much public support and was shocked by the reality of their unpopularity. Those who took up the option to criticise the government found themselves imprisoned or executed whilst Mao decided to radicalism in government policies (Starr, 2001, p.59). The Great Leap Forward was designed to advance Chinese industrial and agricultural output; it was intended to be a major stepping stone on the path the modernisation. In reality it was an economic and humanitarian disaster and caused a man made famine almost without parallel. Although the Great Leap Forward did not damage the Chinese Communist Party fatally in a political sense it was abandoned in 1960. The parallel with the failures of Stalin's industrialisation and collectivisation programmes were uncanny (Wong, 2000, p. 15). As in the Soviet Union three decades earlier it led to a devastating famine, and similar to Stalin, Mao considered that his authority would greatly benefit from beginning a brutal purge (Chang and Halliday, 2006 p. 592).

The end of the Great Leap Forward had not lessened the desire of Mao and the more radical members of the CCP leadership to modernise China through radical cultural, political and economic changes. The search for radical approaches to the modernisation of China would lead to the period when the relationship between the ideas of the May 4th Movement, the New Culture Movement and the CCP would be at their strongest, during the Cultural Revolution. In many respects the Cultural Revolution would be the Chinese equivalent of the Stalinist purges. The Cultural Revolution was intended to increase the control of the CCP and Mao over the country. The aim of the Cultural Revolution was to reduce the influence of technocrats and the intelligentsia on Chinese culture and society. The Cultural Revolution would reverse one of the CCP's most meaningful achievements, the extension of education to all. Communist rule has also expanded the number of university students and supplied China with the doctors, teachers and engineers etc needed for effective modernisation. Forcing the best trained and best educated people to work in the state owned factories, or collective farms may have fitted with following New Culture Movement concepts of having one dominant culture and the communist notion of making everybody equal but it proved ruinous to China's modernisation (Comfort, 1993, p.139).

The simple explanation of the Cultural Revolution was that Mao did not trust technocrats, high-ranking party bureaucrats or university students and their professors. Mao regarded workers and peasants on the other hand as being the regime's and the country's strongest foundation and the key to modernisation (Wong, 2000, p.97). Former students formed into the Red Guard carried the Cultural Revolution forward and the Chinese Army went around the country removing any visible signs of foreign, capitalist or intellectual influence. They regarded the Cultural Revolution as a great cleansing of China. They were guided in their cleansing obey the 'Quotations from Chairman Mao' or the Little Red Book (Wakin, 1997, pp.33-34).

The Cultural Revolution was highly destructive as it disrupted the effective management of the economy and produced political instability. The hysteria and xenophobia that resulted from the Cultural Revolution may have resembled the attitudes or beliefs of the May 4th Movement and the NCM yet in the end they would undermine Mao's position within the CCP and China itself. The Cultural Revolution produced the logical outcome that could have been easily predicted and thus prevented, huge drop in factory and farm production. Even before Mao died the situation had to be reversed. Those technocrats, party bureaucrats and intellectuals that had survived the Cultural Revolution were restored to their former positions or given new ones. Mao successors attempted to further modernise China by producing economic reforms that amounted to capitalism in all but name whilst maintaining a tight grip on China's cultural and political development (Eatwell & Wright, 2003, p.119). China's economic growth and development has been remarkable since the 1970s yet this resulted from abandoning the state planned command economy and letting managers and businesses get on with running things. China introduced the economic reforms later attempted in the Soviet Union and in Central and Eastern Europe. The main difference was that the CCP did not abandon its tight political controls whereas the Soviet Union collapsed after the CPSU abandoned its. In many respects history has turned full circle, the CCP is widely seen as corrupt and ineffective just like the Imperial dynasty and the Kuomintang regime. For many Chinese its only saving grace is that it provides the stability that allows them to grow richer. Should they doubt the importance of stability they can always compare themselves to Russia and most of the other Soviet republics since 1991 (Starr, 2001, p. 59).

Therefore it can be concluded that were relationships between the May 4th Movement, the New Culture Movement and the CCP that contributed to the modernisation of China. These relationships varied in their strength, influence and intensity according to the situations the CCP found itself in and which views dominated the party at any given time. The main influence that the May 4th Movement had in its relationship with the CCP was that it stressed that China had to modernise to free herself of foreign interference and invaders. The May 4th Movement influenced not only the CCP but also it's former allies and bitterest rivals, the Kuomintang endowing both with a strong sense of nationalism. In many ways once the CCP gained power it fulfilled the May 4th Movement's aims of making China a strong modernised country that did not easily give in to foreign demands or pressure. Mao may have used Soviet aid and advisors yet he needed them to rebuild and modernise China just as the Soviet Union had been modernised. The Soviet influence decreased as Mao became more confident of his success and after they stopped supporting the Great Leap

Forward. The time that the New Culture Movement had its strongest relationship with the CCP was during the Cultural Revolution. That was when Mao aimed to make everybody China culturally uniform and economically equal by making the more skilled workers and bureaucrats work in factories and on farms rather than doing the jobs they were trained to do.

Bibliography

Brendon, P (2000) Dark Valley – A Panorama of the 1930s, Jonathan Cape, London

Chang J and Halliday J, (2006) Mao – The Unknown Story, Vintage Books, London

Comfort, N (1993) Brewer's Politics – A Phase and Fable Dictionary

Dikotter F, (2010) Mao's Great Famine – The History of China's Most Devastating Catastrophe, 1958 -62, Bloomsbury, London, New Delhi, New York and Sydney

Eatwell R and Wright, R (2003) Contemporary Political Ideologies, 2nd edition, Continuum, London

Evans, G and Newnham, J (1998) Dictionary of International Relations, Penguin, London

Fraser, D (1990) Collins Concise Dictionary of Quotations, Harper Collins Publishers, London

Hobsbawm, E (1994) Age of Extremes – The Short Twentieth Century 1914-1991, Michael Joseph, London

Starr, J B (2001) Understanding China, 2nd edition, Profile Books, London

Turner, B - editor (2000) China Profiled, Macmillan, London

Wakin, E (1997) Asian Independence Leaders, Facts on File Inc, New York

Wasserstrom, J N – editor (2003) Routledge, London and New York

Wong, J (1997) Red China Blues, Bantam Books, London

In what ways and with what effects did the politicisation of culture contribute to the Chinese Communist Party's consolidation of power between the 1940s and the mid-1970s?

Mao started clearing the ground for a big purge from the moment the famine abated. He put the brakes on liberal measures such as letting peasants lease some land, and rehabilitating political victims, and he steadily fuelled his personality cult.
(Chang and Halliday, 2006 p. 592).

Introduction

The following will debate and discuss the ways in which the politicisation of Chinese culture contributed to the Chinese Communist Party's consolidating its political position between the 1940s and the mid 1970s. The evaluation will discuss whether the politicisation of Chinese culture by the Chinese Communist Party from the start of the 1940s and the mid 1970s proved to be beneficial for the party's efforts to consolidate its political pre-eminence within China itself. The Chinese Communist Party had deliberately set out to politicise Chinese culture for the reasons examined below. Strong arguments can be made to support the notion that the consolidation of political power by the Chinese Communist Party via its policies to complete the politicisation of culture in China.

The Gaining of Power

To a very large extent Chinese culture was notable for the way in which the politicisation that had taken place had eluded the great majority of the Chinese masses by the early decades of the twentieth century. Any of the politicisation that had taken place was confined to the intelligentsia, the middle classes, and in urban areas (Lenman, 2004 p. 120). However the great bulk of the Chinese population remained uneducated and illiterate peasants.

The vast majority of Chinese peasants stayed living in rural areas with little effort by the political parties to cultivate their support or manipulate their opinions to stop the country being so backward as well as overwhelmingly rural (Hobsbawm, 1994 p. 28). For thousands of years the Chinese governments, the country's ruling classes, and also its intelligentsia had paid little or absolutely no attention to the culture, education, or social attitudes of the peasants that were, and always had been the majority of the population (Roberts, 2003 p. 395).

No attention was paid to the peasants because the peasants were not considered to be of any kind of significance when it came to the social, political, cultural, or indeed the economic development of China (Lenman,

2004 p. 547).
Generations of Chinese governments regarded the peasants as only being suitable for paying taxes, and occasionally serving in the army if wars were being fought or seemed likely to be fought. For the Chinese government, its land-owning classes, its middle classes, and later the majority of political parties and movements there seemed to be very little point in politicising in national culture (Roberts, 2003 p. 396). Politicisation should not take place, as it would in fact not be beneficial for the social, economic, and most importantly the political status quo of the country. Politicised culture would turn out to be politically damaging for China (Woodruff, 2005 p. 310).

To put it basically the general apathy and the high level of ignorance of national and international politics in Chinese popular culture certainly suited the ruling classes as well as the social and economic elites. The only way in which the Imperial dynasty and the subsequent Kuomtang regime had aimed to even vaguely politicise Chinese popular culture was to promote a strong sense of nationalism (Hobsbawm, 1994 p. 15).

The only political party or movement in China that deliberately and methodically set out to politicise popular and mass culture was the Chinese Communist Party.

As far as the Chinese Communist Party was concerned politicising popular Chinese culture was actually the best means of obtaining over all power right across the whole of China and would then allow them to consolidate their hold on power (Lenman, 2004 p. 395). The strategy of politicising mass culture in China to gain and then consolidate power was actually developed by the leader of the Chinese Communist Party, Mao Zedong (Lenman, 2004 p. 508).

Originally the Chinese Communist Party had hoped that it could take power in China by gaining the support of the urban proletariat. Using the urban proletariat it was anticipated as being essential to gaining power, as Karl Marx had predicted that would be the way in which communist regimes would be established and consolidated across the globe. However, even in countries that had high numbers of the urban proletariat such as Britain and Germany had not gained power at all, let alone with the ease that Marx and Engels had predicted. China was certainly not the country that was expected to install a communist regime as a result of a revolution or a coup, not unless the Chinese Communist Party could achieve the impossible (Woodruff, 2005 p. 207).

The Chinese Communist Party looked for inspiration and guidance from the Soviet Union, the world's first communist state which had attempted to carry out massive social, economic, political as well as cultural changes. In Russia, Lenin had taken power via a coup, as the urban proletariat had not

been in a position to carry out a successful revolution. The Soviet Union had attempted to create communism at the same as it created increasing numbers of the urban proletariat. The Soviet regime had also sought to politicise the culture of the state as a means of consolidating its hold on power. Karl Marx had never expected for a revolution to successfully occur in somewhere as backwards as Russia instead of advanced capitalist countries such as Britain, France, Germany, and the United States.

Mao Zedong and the Chinese Communist Party were faced with the mission of gaining and then consolidating power in a country that was very backwards politically, culturally, and economically, even in comparison with the Russia of 1917 (Roberts, 2003 p. 395).

The Consolidating of Power

For Mao Zedong and also for the Chinese Communist Party the campaign to politicise Chinese culture can be traced back to the late 1920s when the party leadership began its efforts to politicise the Chinese peasants in order to undermine and eventually overthrow the Kuomtang regime. China was actually too backward to have an urban proletariat so as far as the Chinese Communist Party was concerned politicising the peasants was the only way forward in their efforts to gain and consolidate power. Given the extraordinarily high levels of illiteracy and ignorance inside the country the Chinese Communist Party had to educate the peasants before it was able to politicise their culture and transform their political behaviour (Lenman, 2004 p. 508).

The Chinese Communist Party had to defeat two enemies before it was able to gain power in China, the Japanese, and the Kuomtang. For a time the Kuomtang had co-operated with the Chinese Communist Party yet that did not last long. The Chinese Communist Party had to take drastic action through the Long March to survive the onslaught of the Kuomtang. Mao changed tack after the Long March; the road to power depended upon the politicisation of the Chinese peasants. The politicisation of the peasants by the Chinese Communist Party helped them to defeat the Japanese, and then assisted their victory in the resulting civil war. The Chinese Communist Party had only been able to politicise culture in the provinces that it had controlled. Winning the civil war meant that its leadership was able to politicise culture across the whole of the country (Chang and Halliday, 2006 p. 288).

For the Chinese Communist Party there were sound ideological and political reasons for politicising the national culture within China.

As already noted the Chinese Communist Party gained power by winning the Chinese civil war. However winning the civil war did not automatically mean that the party had consolidated its power over the whole of China.

Mao and the Chinese Communist Party wanted to politicise Chinese culture in order to vindicate and justify their seizure of power. However in the 1940s the majority of the Chinese population did not seem to understand the aims and the objectives of the Chinese Communist Party to transform China into a Maoist state. After all Mao regarded the politicisation of Chinese culture as being essential if the population was to fully participate in the transformation of China into a Marxist state that was both modernised and secure. Politicising Chinese culture was used to reinforce the impact and the influence of the Chinese Communist Party policies and also its propaganda. Politicisation consolidated the Chinese Communist Party's position as it made it easier for the party to indoctrinate the Chinese population (http://cid-a2584c236d1c21b2.skydrive.live.com/browse.aspx/Study%20Area/Introduction%20to%20Contemporary%20Chinese%20Societies%20and%20Cultures).

Conclusions

The politicisation of Chinese culture enabled the Chinese Communist Party to legitimate its claims to govern the country from one generation to succeeding generations between the 1940s and the mid 1970s. Although the Chinese Communist Party politicised the culture of China to increase its hold over the entire population it also meant that the party was linked with its Chairman, Mao. For the politicised population Mao was the Chinese Communist Party as well as being their leader whose thoughts and guidance were always available within his little red book. The Chinese Communist Party managed to portray Mao as being the all-powerful and the all-knowing leader of the Chinese people.

Politicisation succeeded in making the Chinese people regard Mao as being the architect of communist China as well as modernising the country and ridding it of mass ignorance. Yet it came at an enormous cost in terms of mass suffering and millions of deaths especially as a consequence of both the Great Leap Forward and later on the Cultural Revolution.

Bibliography

Chang J and Halliday J, (2006) Mao – The Unknown Story, Vintage Books, London

Hobsbawm, E (1994) Age of Extremes, the Short Twentieth Century 1914-1991, Michael Joseph, London

Lenman B P, (2004) Chambers Dictionary of World History - 2nd edition, Chambers, Edinburgh

Roberts J A G (2003) the Complete History of China, Sutton Publishing, London

Woodruff W, (2005) A Concise History of the Modern World, Abacus, London

http://cid-a2584c236d1c21b2.skydrive.live.com/browse.aspx/Study%20Area/Introduction%20to%20Contemporary%20Chinese%20Societies%20and%20Cultures

Printed in Great Britain
by Amazon

71177652R00047